About the author

Founding member of Solmanc_____te Romania, licensed teacher o_ _____ Tango and Fitness, Japanese Tea Ceremony and martial arts instructor, Alexandru Eugen Cristea has a solid background in social interactions and making people see beyond their confort zone in order to reach their full potential.

Other books by this author

Tarot Restitutio (co-author)

Gurdjieffian exercises

Gurdjieff's Human Types

Gurdjieff's The Three Bodies of Man

Gurdjieff Movements, Vol. 1 – 4

Enneagram Applications, Vol. 1 & 2

Tango Lessons

Tango for Teachers, Vol. 1 – 3

Tarraxinha

Kizomba 100 Elements (co-author)

Alexandru Eugen Cristea

Transdisciplinary Coaching with Tarot

Transdisciplinary Coaching, Vol. 1

- Transdisciplinary Coaching with Tarot by Alexandru Eugen Cristea -

Publisher: Magisteria

Bucharest, 2017

Copyright for the present edition © Magisteria 2017

Cover design: Iulius Fotin

Table of contents

Preface .... - 1 -
Introduction .... - 2 -
Transdisciplinary Coaching .... - 4 -
   What is coaching? .... - 5 -
      Types of Coaching .... - 8 -
      Coaching Models .... - 9 -
         How to GROW .... - 9 -
         Ishikawa Diagram .... - 12 -
      The Coaching Relationship .... - 14 -
      Coaching Strategies .... - 18 -
         Silence .... - 19 -
         Listening .... - 19 -
         Contract .... - 20 -
         Body language .... - 20 -
         Questions .... - 20 -
         Shifting .... - 22 -
         Feedback .... - 22 -
   What is Transdisciplinarity? .... - 24 -
      The Methodology .... - 27 -
      The first axiom .... - 28 -
      The second axiom .... - 29 -
      The third axiom .... - 30 -
      The Delors report .... - 31 -
   Transdisciplinary Coaching .... - 33 -
      I see Levels .... - 34 -
         How to begin .... - 35 -
         Body, Mind, Emotion .... - 36 -
         Individual, Social, Cosmic .... - 36 -
      I see Contradictions .... - 38 -
         Alignments .... - 41 -
         Unity, Complexity, Simple-ness .... - 41 -
         Status .... - 42 -
         The Six Processes .... - 43 -
      I see Relationships .... - 45 -
         Masculine and Feminine .... - 45 -
         The Dramatic Triangle .... - 47 -
         Obedience .... - 50 -
         Team Coaching .... - 51 -

- Tarot .... - 53 -
  - What's with the Tarot? .... - 54 -
    - Short History .... - 54 -
    - The Tarot Deck .... - 55 -
    - Knowledge by Numbers .... - 56 -
  - The Major Arcana .... - 57 -
    - Le Mat .... - 58 -
    - Le Bateleur .... - 60 -
    - La Papesse .... - 62 -
    - L'Impératrice .... - 64 -
    - L'Empereur .... - 66 -
    - Le Pape .... - 68 -
    - L'Amoureux .... - 70 -
    - Le Chariot .... - 72 -
    - La Justice .... - 74 -
    - L'Ermite .... - 76 -
    - La Roue de Fortune .... - 78 -
    - La Force .... - 80 -
    - Le Pendu .... - 82 -
    - Sin Nom .... - 84 -
    - Tempérance .... - 86 -
    - Le Diable .... - 88 -
    - La Maison Dieu .... - 90 -
    - L'Étoile .... - 92 -
    - La Lune .... - 94 -
    - Le Soleil .... - 96 -
    - Le Jugement .... - 98 -
    - Le Monde .... - 100 -
    - Review of the Major Arcana .... - 102 -
      - Big and small .... - 102 -
      - The look .... - 102 -
  - How to Spread .... - 104 -
    - Rules for Reading .... - 104 -
    - Basic Spreads .... - 105 -
    - How to Choose .... - 111 -
- Transdisciplinary Coaching with Tarot .... - 112 -
  - Where to begin .... - 113 -
    - Illustrating the situation .... - 113 -
      - The Two Endings .... - 113 -
      - Building bridges vs. Burning bridges .... - 114 -
      - Human Map .... - 116 -
      - The GROW model .... - 118 -

    The Dramatic Triangle - revisited .... - 120 -
Extracting meaning .... - 128 -
    Translating into symbols .... - 129 -
    Frame of reference .... - 130 -
    A Dialogue in Images .... - 131 -
    The Map and the Territory .... - 132 -
Conclusion .... - 134 -

Preface

Coaching has become a new religion over the years and a lot of branches and special types of coaching appear nowadays, producing more and more complexion and digression in a world full of details but lacking the general view needed in order to orient oneself in the unknown grounds of the everyday life.

I consider the Transdisciplinary approach as the key to the coaching experience, regardless of the type of coaching in question.

The "game" and cards of Tarot have been around since the world began to tell us about the very same universal truths that govern the human being: the psychological and emotional aspects without which the contemporary man would be just another empty shell.

This book will present a fresh view of the Tarot and its symbols, teaching the reader how to use the Tarot cards in the Transdisciplinary coaching process, with a client, both in life and business coaching, in order to facilitate a deeper understanding and a broader view on the present life.

The Tarot cards – in this approach – are used just like a psychological tool – like any other coaching tool available on the market, for both the coaching specialist and the mere beginner.

Alexandru Eugen Cristea

1st of November 2017

Introduction

To use the Tarot cards only as a tool for predicting the future is not only to underestimate their value and minimize their potential to transmit ancient truths about the human psyche, but also to imagine that the prediction of the future is possible by such means.

In this book I will give a simple and powerful description of what coaching is and how one should use it – in life and business coaching – and then present the Tarot cards, with their symbols and meanings – as related to our subject.

Most of the information about the Tarot cards presented here is not to be found in other books available on the market, with one notable exception[1]. The coaching through Tarot approach is unique.

> *Transdisciplinarity* connotes a research strategy that crosses many disciplinary boundaries to create a holistic approach. As the prefix "trans" indicates, transdisciplinarity concerns that which is at once between the disciplines, across the different disciplines, and beyond each individual discipline. Its goal is the understanding of the present world, of which one of the imperatives is the overarching unity of knowledge.[2]

---

[1] Adrian Mirel Petrariu, *The Mythology of the Energy*: Transdisciplinarity, the Force of Gurdjieff and the Tarot, Magisteria, 2015.
[2] https://en.wikipedia.org/wiki/Transdisciplinarity

Throughout this book, we will use the three methodological postulates of Basarab Nicolescu[3] as practical coaching tools and with the aid of the symbols in the Tarot cards we will present to the reader a comprehensive approach to coaching.

---

[3] Basarab Nicolescu, *Transdisciplinarity – Theory and Practice* (Ed.), Hampton Press, Cresskill, NJ, USA, 2008.

Transdisciplinary Coaching

What is coaching?

According to numerous studies and coach masters, the process is quite simple in its essence: it is about how to coach another person or group of persons so that a specific aim is achieved.

Just like a tennis coach does not play the game for the other person, in the same way a coach does not apply the solution for the other person.

Coaching is a form of development in which a person called a coach supports a learner or client in achieving a specific personal or professional goal by providing training and guidance.[1] The learner is sometimes called a coachee. Occasionally, coaching may mean an informal relationship between two people, of whom one has more experience and expertise than the other and offers advice and guidance as the latter learns; but coaching differs from mentoring in focusing on specific tasks or objectives, as opposed to more general goals or overall development.[4]

In many a cases, the coach does not even give the solution, but only creates the necessary atmosphere for the other person to reach

---

[4] https://en.wikipedia.org/wiki/Coaching

his/her own conclusion. From this perspective, a coach is a creator of different types of *mise en scène*, specific to the client's needs.

As any other profession, coaching has some DO's and DON'Ts but since each client is different, some person's DO's are another person's DON'Ts. The coach will have to be able to identify each case needs, create and apply the required strategy.

Although sometimes the coach is seen as a mentor, a friend, a solution-giver or a teacher, the professional coach is something more than all of the above. If we consider the above mentioned as separate disciplines, the coach will be transdisciplinary oriented: he is able to be any of the above but also much more.

There are some qualities that good coaches have and some of them can be found in the next illustration.

Professional coaching uses a range of communication skills (such as targeted restatements, listening, questioning, clarifying etc.) to help clients shift their perspectives and thereby discover different approaches to achieve their goals.[5]

In what will follow, I will present some basic information about the coaching process, from the point of view of the coach, and some key points to be observed in practice.

---

[5] Cox, Elaine (2013), *Coaching Understood: a Pragmatic Inquiry into the Coaching Process*, Los Angeles; London: Sage Publications, ISBN 9780857028259, OCLC 805014954.

Types of Coaching

There are a many types of coaching available on the market, and usually they differ by their purpose or field of application:
- Life coaching.
- Business coaching.
- Career coaching.
- ADHD coaching[6].
- Health and wellness coaching.
- Relationship coaching.
- Sports coaching.
- Etc.

As the reader can notice, most of the types of coaching listed above are self-explanatory, at least at the first glance. We can consider most of them as being single-discipline based, like ADHD coaching or multidiscipline based, like life coaching, health and wellness coaching, etc.

In order to understand the transition from something on the horizontal level – interdisciplinary and multidisciplinary – to something on the vertical level – transdisciplinarity – please read the next chapter.

In what follows, we will present some basic coaching models, or tools, for the reader to grasp the coaching process better.

---

[6] attention-deficit hyperactivity disorder.

Coaching Models

How to GROW

We are now entering the world of classical coaching and its tools: different strategies, models and applications.

The GROW Model is deservedly one of the most established and successful coaching models. Created by Sir John Whitmore and colleagues in the 1980s, it was popularized in Sir John's best-selling book, Coaching for Performance.[7]

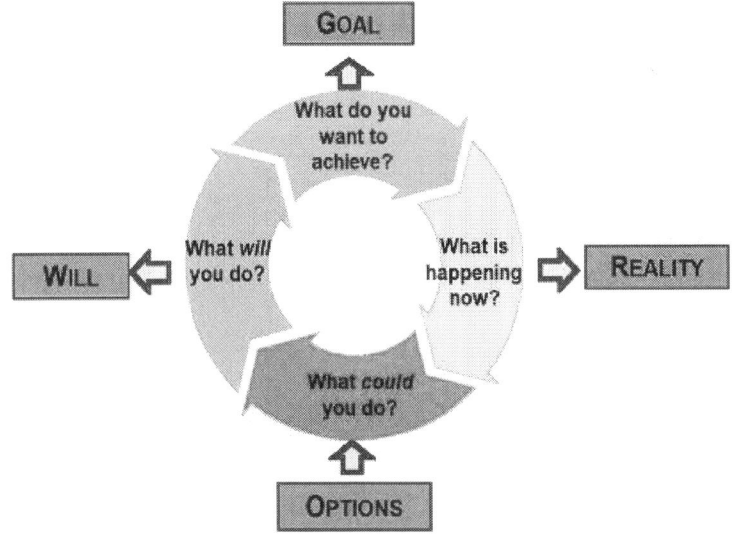

---
[7] https://www.performanceconsultants.com/grow-model

The GROW model is one of the simplest strategies for problem solving and goal setting and this is what makes it so good. The important part of this model is for the coach to facilitate the client's ability to answer and commit to the above four stages of development and guide the client along the way.

If the first two stages – Goal and Reality – are more client oriented – because the client wants something achieved in his/her world, the other two stages – Options and Will – are more oriented towards the coach.

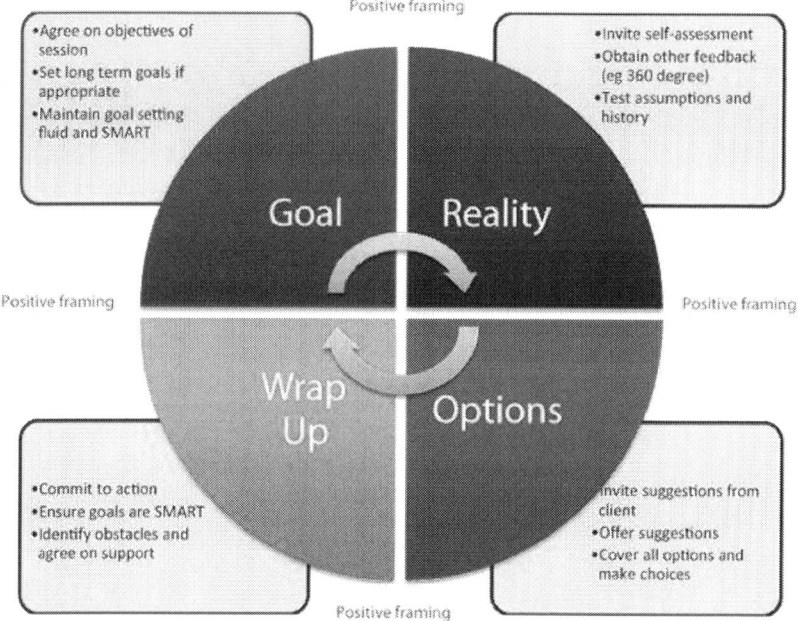

A common practice is for the coach to enable the client to see more options and suggest different strategies to the client so that the goal will be achieved.

However, as I have already mentioned, the best practice is to empower the client to find the required solution.

In the illustration above, SMART stands for: Specific, Measurable, Achievable, Relevant, Time-bound.

Other similar models for decision making have been implemented in different fields for a long time with excellent results:
- PDCA (Plan – Do – Check – Act) in quality control.
- GOFER (Goals – Options – Facts – Effects - Review) for adolescents.
- OODA (Observe – Orient – Decide – Act) in the USA army.

Now that we have a better representation of a coaching model, let's see what makes it so special.

First of all, the GROW tool *can be used in many types of situations* as most of the clients want something to be achieved. Whether it is in their personal life – as in life coaching – or in their company or business – as in career coaching or business coaching – in 80% of the cases, this tool can be used with great success as a starter. If the situation is more complex, it will require advanced tools, but the bottom line could still be assessed using the GROW model.

Secondly, *the proportion between what is clear and what is vague* doesn't bother the client or the coach. It is clear enough to be used, but the tool itself does not impose anything – any particular direction to be followed.

And last but not the least, the tool has *more than two dimensions*, or steps, or areas. This is quite important as strategies with only two stages "either this or that" are most of the time a terrible choice of action. The fact that there are four dimensions of space means, in the broader view of the concept, that there will be four aspects to any given situation. The reader will understand this better in the second part of the book, where we talk specifics.

The same three things mentioned above must be valid for any tool used in coaching, for any model, for any perspective, in order to obtain positive results.

Ishikawa Diagram

One very useful tool is the cause and effect diagram developed by Kaoru Ishikawa in 1960s, thus becoming a key-figure in modern management.

The causes should be grouped under different categories, such us:

1) The 6 Ms: Men/people, machines, methods, materials, measures, mother nature.
2) 4 Ps - Places, Procedures, People, Politics.
3) 4 Ss - Surroundings, Suppliers, Systems, Skills.

Here we can see an application[8] of this concept:

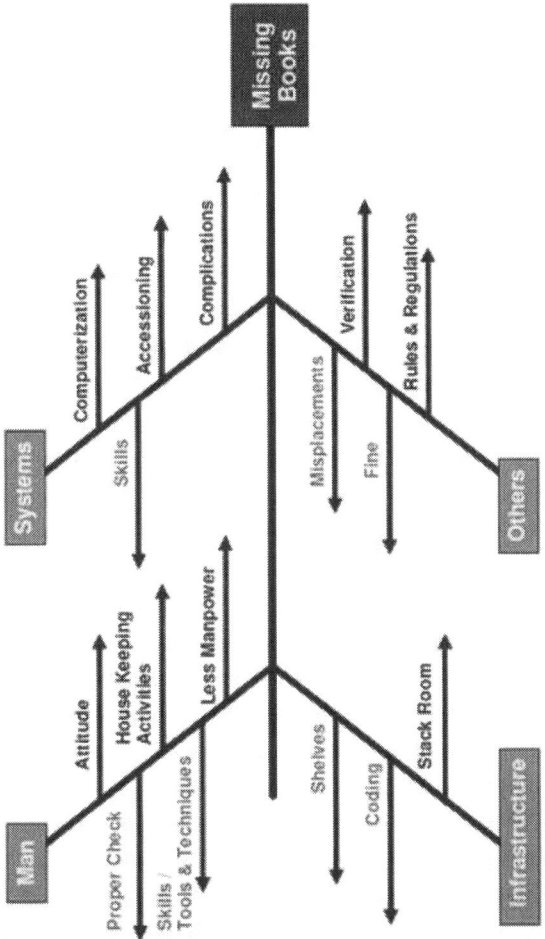

---
[8] http://www.whatishumanresource.com/cause-and-effect-diagram-or-fish-bone-diagram-or-ishikawa-diagram

The Coaching Relationship

An important part of the coaching process is the relationship between the coach and the client (coachee). The relationship has to be as transparent as possible, with both parties understanding the role of the other and not stepping over. A professional contract is used most of the times with clear points agreed upon.

But the relationship will have to be developed from the very start, and this will usually mean some type of a document that the coach sends to the client – future client – in order for the client to understand the general coordinates of the commitment. This document needs not be as detailed as a contract, but has to have the necessary amount of detail so that the client will understand the general approach of the coach.

Next, after this preliminary action, there will be the first meeting face to face between the coach and the possible future client.

At this meeting all the coaching strategies that are described in the next chapter are valid and the coach will have to use them efficiently in order to establish rapport.

By far the most important abilities of the coach at this point will be to know how to listen and how to ask relevant questions in order to understand the needs of the possible future client.

Presence and awareness are required and from a certain point beyond, negotiating skills.

Tarot

At the first meeting, or soon after, the coach and the client will have to sign an *initial contract*, which will have most of the important details about how long will the relationship between the coach and the client be, what are the client's objectives to be achieved, the relationship's frame, the type of coaching involved, the price per session, etc.

There should be no practical action from the coach before the signing of this initial contract.

> This initial contract first serves to position each coach in his or her specific frame of reference and second to limit the scope of the professional relationship and thereby protect all the contracting partners[9].

---

[9] http://www.metasysteme-coaching.eu/english/toolbox-iii-client-agreement-skills-in-coaching/

Beyond the initial contract, which will remain the most formal one, with legal implications, there will be other type of contracts to be negotiated and applied. The *contract concept* is one of the basic strategies in coaching and a practical tool to be used at different levels of interaction, as we will see in the next chapter.

The coaching relationship will change as the coaching sessions develop and these changes will have to be acknowledged by both the coach and the client, through awareness and dialogue. The general frame of reference will remain, but details will sometimes be re-negotiated.

As already mentioned, the coach is to be seen as a guide who accompanying the client and the solution in any situation should be the result of both the coach and the client, not information coming from the coach.

The ability to give and receive feedback is an important part of the coaching relationship, and also a practical strategic tool, that will be covered in the next chapter as well. This ability has an emotional[10] impact and connects the formulation of the client's objective and the moment when the objectives are achieved. And bearing in mind that the main objective is achieved by many small objectives, the feedback and assessment of quality and goal achieving will be an important part of each coaching session.

---

[10] A. M. Petrariu, On *Emotions*, Magisteria, 2017.

Coaching Strategies

In this chapter we will see a brief presentation about coaching strategies, that is, those apparently small things that the coach needs to be able to do in order to master the relationship with the client.

All these strategies are common things in the everyday life, but simply knowing about them does not mean that we can apply them. Also, there is an important difference to be made between an act in everyday life and an act in a coaching session and the difference lies in the fact that in the coaching session there is always an objective, an aim to be accomplished. Using a simple rule of a thumb and a famous quote from G. I. Gurdjieff, we can posit that *an action is **good** if it takes us closer to the goal and an action is **bad** if it takes us in the opposite direction.*

In order to be able to do what we have just explained, any coach should be able to split his attention simultaneous in at least three directions:

- The goal to be achieved as per the initial contract.
- The dialogue with the client at that particular moment.
- The strategy to be applied.

Without digressing too much into the spiritual dimension of the implications of the above statement[11] and without presenting practical exercises[12] for this ability to be achieved as it is not the aim of this book,

---

[11] Alexandru Eugen Cristea, *Gurdjieff's Three Bodies of Man*, Magisteria, 2017.
[12] Alexandru Eugen Cristea, *Gurdjieffian exercises,* Magisteria, 2014.

we will continue to present those simple, yet powerful strategies that the coach should use in the interaction with the client.

Silence

In order for the client to speak, the client needs to have the space to do so, and this should be achieved by the silence from the coach.

This is the main tool used in coaching, the silence that creates a frame or the client to manifest in order to express his understanding and goals.

The silence of the coach should be an active one, induced by the coach so that it would not bring about unpleasant emotions from the client such as boredom, nervousness, haste, etc.

Listening

The art of listening is very important and the way to do this is by being able to listen without searching for an answer or a reply at the same time.

The coach should be able to repeat the gist of the client's words or the exact words after listening.

The active listening of the client should sometimes be guided by relevant and strategic questions that will open up the client more towards the goal to be achieved.

Contract

The coach should understand that each session is a negotiating ground and at the end of each session the client should clearly understand what is to be done.

There are numerous types of agreements or contracts, informal, without anything being written down, that the coach and the client will adhere to: session agreements, sequence agreements, homework agreements, etc. All these will be in the same line with the initial contract and will have the same objective: to attain the goal initially negotiated with the client.

Body language

There is a lot of information available on this subject, so I will only give a few hints: the posture of the body, the tone of voice and the gestures are very important, and so is the nodding of the head, the blinking of the eyes and the verbal nodding such as: "Yes...", "I see...", "Um...", etc.

Questions

The coach should be able to ask relevant questions and also know what type of questions to use.

The questions should be introduced by asking permission, such as "Can I interrupt you with a question?"

There are close questions (with a yes/ no answer) or open questions, where the answer will be longer and more detailed. Also there are guided questions, or neutral; etc.

There is also a specific form of questioning by repeating the last word/s used by the client so that the client will provide more information regarding that topic.

The coach should also perceive the key-words used by the client, those words that the clients repeats, and use them in the dialogue with the client.

Empowering the client means to create the necessary frame so that the client will assume some responsibility towards the goal to be achieved. Questions such as "What do you want to achieve today?" are useful for this purpose.

The coach should avoid questions such as "why?" because of the client will most of the time simply repeat what has been already said.

Shifting

Shifting the frame for a few moments in order for the client to grasp a new point of view is sometimes quite useful.

The coach can choose to *shift the time frame* – by using questions such as "What would the future look with the problem already solved?", or "Have you solved problems such as this in the past?" – or *shift the place frame* – "What would you do in his/ her place?".

Feedback

The ability to give and receive feedback is very important as it stands in direct connection with the achieving of the client's goal.

The coach should always ask for permission before giving feedback, and the client should also be encouraged to give feedback after each session and after each small goal achieved as part of the achievement of the bigger goal.

As the word itself describes, by feedback we are actually feeding the relationship with the client. Most of the time, the client will not have the initiative to give feedback, so this will have to be developed in the session.

There are numerous strategies to be observed and any regular coach should be aware of these above mentioned things.

What is Transdisciplinarity?

The word itself was first introduced by the Swiss psychologist Jean Piaget in at a seminar on interdisciplinarity in universities held at the University of Nice.

Jack Lee Mahan, Jr., in his doctoral dissertation, *Toward Transdisciplinary Inquiry in the Humane Sciences*, in the same year 1970, independently of Jean Piaget, wrote about it:

> Transdisciplinary inquiry would be characterized by a common orientation to transcend disciplinary boundaries and an attempt to bring continuity to inquiry and knowledge. Other characteristics would be: attention to comprehensiveness, context and frame of reference of inquiry and knowledge; interpenetration of boundaries between concepts and disciplines; exposing disciplinary boundaries to facilitate understanding of implicit assumptions, processes of inquiry, and resulting knowledge; humanistic reverence for life and human dignity; desire to actively apply knowledge to the betterment of man and society.[13]

What we can easily understand from this, is the need of the emergence of the word and of its content. In order to better understand

---

[13] Jack Lee Mahan, *Toward Transdisciplinary Inquiry in the Humane Sciences*, 1970, page 194.

it, let's see what the other words similar to it have as content and then proceed to deepen our understanding and knowledge.

Multidisciplinarity is about looking at a certain topic from the point of view of another discipline; studying that particular topic in this way.

Interdisciplinarity is about transferring of methods from one discipline to another.

Transdisciplinarity is about that which is at the same time between disciplines, across them and beyond them.

> There is no opposition between disciplinarity (including multidisciplinarity and interdisciplinarity) and transdisciplinarity, but there is instead a fertile complementarity. In fact, there is no transdisciplinarity without disciplinarity.[14]

The goal of transdisciplinarity is the understanding of the world in which we live, and this cannot be done by limiting ourselves to one discipline or event to any number of disciplines, as the unity of knowledge is something that needs to permeate through all our contacts with the reality around us.

In what follows, we shall see more about the methodology of transdisciplinarity and then apply this to coaching.

---

[14] http://www.basarab-nicolescu.fr/Docs_Notice/TJESNo_1_12_2010.pdf, page 4.

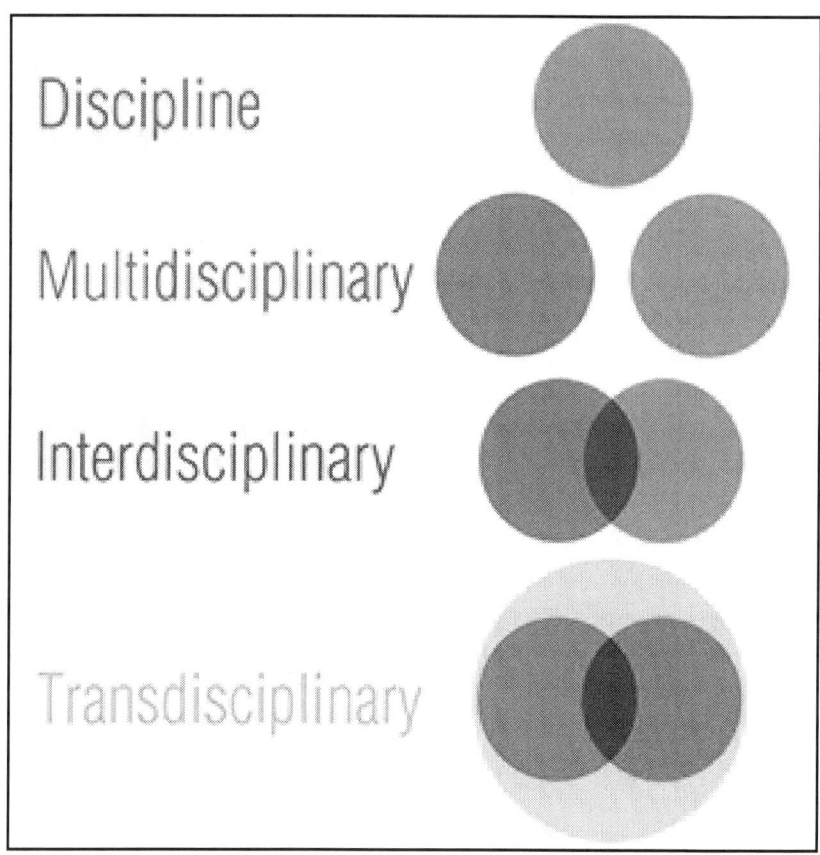

The Methodology

The most important part of the transdisciplinarity is its axiomatic[15] methodology, which is formulated[16] as follows:

> 1. The ontological axiom: There are, in Nature and society and in our knowledge of Nature and society, different levels of Reality of the Object and, correspondingly, different levels of Reality of the Subject.
>
> 2. The logical axiom: The passage from one level of Reality to another is ensured by the logic of the included middle.
>
> 3. The complexity axiom: The structure of the totality of levels of Reality or perception is a complex structure: every level is what it is because all the levels exist at the same time.

Without going too much into detail, as it is not the aim of this book, I shall give a few details about each of the three axioms, so that the reader will understand the departing point, and then proceed to the application in coaching. I strongly advise the reader to go deeper into transdisciplinarity, as a key to the understanding of our existence and of the relationship between us and the world around us.

---

[15] self-evident or unquestionable.
[16] Basarab Nicolescu, 1996.

The first axiom

The levels of Reality have to do with different systems with different laws. The laws that work in the social field do not apply in the mathematical field, or in the medical field.

These fields are separate levels of the same Reality, with a discontinuity between them. If there is no discontinuity, there would not be different levels, and no different laws.

Moreover, there is a different space-time in each level of Reality and one cannot understand Reality from the point of view of one level only as no level is fundamental, but incomplete.

The principle of relativity works here, as one level of reality is what it is because all the other levels around it are what they are, so in order to know about a certain topic we must also know about other topics.

> Knowledge is neither exterior nor interior; it is simultaneously exterior and interior. The studies of the universe and of the human being sustain one another. Without spirituality, the knowledge is a dead knowledge.[17]

---

[17] http://www.basarab-nicolescu.fr/Docs_Notice/TJESNo_1_12_2010.pdf, page 11.

The second axiom

The logic of the included middle has to do with the contradictions one encounters while travelling n the same level of Reality. As Gödel suggested, one is bound to find incomplete things or contradictory things, and when doing so, the logic of the included middle will apply in order to pass from one level of Reality to another.

The reader should keep in mind that the classical logic where there will never exist *a third term* which is *at the same time* A and non-A does not apply here, as it does not apply in quantum physics.

Stéphane Lupasco (1900-1988) is the person who has shown that the logic of the *included* middle – as opposed to the classical *excluded* middle – is a veritable logic, non-contradictory.

In order to better understand this, we will require the previous axiom, that of the levels of Reality, so that we can affirm the existence of an third term, which is at the same time A and non-A, but in a different level of Reality than A and non-A.

Of course, the logic of the included middle does not exclude the logic of the excluded middle; both laws govern different areas.

> The included middle logic is a tool for an integrative process: it allows us to cross two different levels of Reality or of perception and to effectively integrate, not

only in thinking but also in our own being, the coherence of the Universe.[18]

The third axiom

This axiom should be somewhat easy to understand: no thing exists isolated. In order to exist, one must exchange with the other existing things. All live systems are open – in the sense of communication and exchange. In other words, there is an universal interdependence and there is no possibility to ignore this, as only dead systems are not under this law.

We should also be aware of the point of view when we talk about complexity: there will be at least two directions: horizontal and vertical.

> It is therefore useful to distinguish between the horizontal complexity, which refers to a single level of reality and vertical complexity, which refers to several levels of Reality.[19]

---

[18]http://www.basarab-nicolescu.fr/Docs_Notice/TJESNo_1_12_2010.pdf, page 13.
[19]http://www.basarab-nicolescu.fr/Docs_Notice/TJESNo_1_12_2010.pdf, page 14.

The Delors report

We cannot finish our basic presentation of Transdisciplinarity without saying a few words about education in general and the transdisciplinary approach, so evident in the Delors[20] report.

The four pillars of education stated in the report are of utmost importance in our present and future education, and the coaching approach to life in general and solving problems in particular should always refer back to these pillars:

1) Learning to know – a broad general knowledge with the opportunity to work in depth on a small number of subjects.
2) Learning to do – to acquire not only occupational skills but also the competence to deal with many situations and to work in teams.
3) Learning to be – to develop one's personality and to be able to act with growing autonomy, judgment and personal responsibility.
4) Learning to live together – by developing an understanding of other people and an appreciation of interdependence[21].

---

[20] the eighth President of the European Commission.
[21] https://en.wikipedia.org/wiki/Delors_Report

In what follows, we shall see hot to apply the transdisciplinary methodology and attitude to the coaching process as a basis for the transdisciplinary coaching.

Transdisciplinary Coaching

In what will follow I will present some basic guidelines for this new approach: the transdisciplinary coaching. But the best way to start is with the next posit made by one of the founders of transdisciplinary coaching, Adrian Mirel Petrariu, Ph. D.

> Transdisciplinary Coaching does not work with concrete problems, for that is the task of disciplinary coaching. In fact, the very concept of "problem" involves a mistake, as well as the *success-failure* trap, while we insist on the idea of alternatives. Transdisciplinary Coaching can provide assistance in changing the attitude one has towards life with a new attitude that can offer an alternative life experience[22].

As we can easily understand, Transdisciplinary Coaching is about applying the concepts of transdisciplinarity into coaching, and the main concepts that we will apply are the levels of reality, the hidden third and the interdependence of all that exists.

Of course, this is only the starting point in our endeavor, as the aim of this book is to acquaint the reader with the use of the symbols of the Tarot cards in a coaching session, which will be the topic of our next two chapters after the guidelines of how the Transdisciplinary Coaching functions.

---

[22]https://www.facebook.com/groups/429734087217014/permalink/763370480520038/

I see Levels

In respect to any person that wants a coaching session, that person will be in one of the following situations:
- to acquire something that does not have.
- to become something that is not.

As space has four dimensions, the two situations above have their two correspondents in the "negative":
- to get rid of something that one has.
- to stop being in a certain way.

Needless to say, each of these four possibilities is, in a certain way, the "solution" to the other, and because one of the first goals of Transdisciplinary Coaching is to make the client see more options and a change in the weltanschauung[23], the coach should be able to guide the client in discovering these four possibilities by himself/ herself.

Adrian Mirel Petrariu posits that:

> The confusion of levels of stupidity makes humans ignore the principle of gradation between the levels of the world.
>
> Failing therefore to see that there are degrees of good and evil, they thing good is the same everywhere and because of that the good in Hell is the same good as in Heaven, while the reality is very different: what is evil

---

[23] A world view or worldview is the fundamental cognitive orientation of an individual or society encompassing the whole of the individual's or society's knowledge and point of view (Wikipedia).

in Heaven is becoming more and more good as descending through the levels, because the evil is getting in its turn more and more diabolical and what is good in Heaven becomes more and more impossible while descending through the levels.

This blindness and confusion also makes humans perceive selfcalming in front of evil as "optimism", as "seeing the good in everything" is actually "reducing all levels of good to a single, imaginary one", preventing them forever to reach real optimism, which is not imaginary, but the reality of trying the impossible as aspiring maximally towards the highest good, being also perfectly aware it's impossible[24].

How to begin

The very first thing one has to understand is how to begin, how to search, how to learn to see.

And here we must posit that in order to have a correct answer, we must use three simultaneous directions: information, experience, observation.

In other words, each information that one receives, from any source, should be tested against reality, in an experience that has to do with that particular information, and while having that experience, one should observe, as objective as possible, what is happening.

---

[24] https://www.facebook.com/solmancer/posts/1731784393796027

This way, the energy[25] that the human being has to understand the world is used in a correct and coherent manner.

Body, Mind, Emotion

One of the first things we need to understand is the existence of three parts in the human being: a physical part – the body, an intellectual part – the mind, and an affective part – the emotions and feelings.

Each of these has its own type of manifestations: sensations for the physical part, thoughts for the intellectual part and emotions and feelings for the affective part. And it is very important to learn how to recognize these emanations and not to mistake one for another if we want to see a clear picture of the human being.

There is a lot of information available on this topic[26], especially in The Force of Gurdjieff Collection.

Individual, Social, Cosmic

In order to understand one level of reality, we need to understand other levels also, and this is most valid in studying the adjacent levels.

From the moment man is born, man lives in three levels at the same time: the individual level, the social level, the cosmic level.

---

[25] Adrian Mirel Petrariu, *The Mythology of the Energy*: Transdisciplinarity, the Force of Gurdjieff and the Tarot, Magisteria, 2015.
[26] Alexandru Eugen Cristea, *Gurdjieff's Human Types*, Magisteria, 2015.

The individual level is about what happens in one's private live, things that have to do with the inside of man – the affective part and the intellectual part – and man taken as a separate human being, an individual.

The social level is about relationship with other people – any type of relationship – and man's place in a bigger group – family, corporation, etc.

The cosmic level has to do with man's destiny, with his place in the world, that most important feature that gives our purpose in life.

I see Contradictions

The energy necessary for manifestation that is inside the human being will always need to manifest and as Gödel demonstrated contradictions will appear.

Each time we face a contradiction, if we will self-calm and go towards one of the contradiction's terms, that is, if we "choose" one, then from 2 elements that we had at the beginning, when we had the contradiction, now we will have only 1 element. And from this 1 element, the only place to go is down to 0.

If we want to go up, to understand more and see the situation from another point of view, we will have to apply the logic of the included third.

> Basically, any form of existence, any phenomenon exists by contradiction and its solution. The importance of the formalization of a phenomenon consisting of itself and its opposite is given by the practical impossibility to understand existence, the construction and structure of a system without clarifying such model.[27]

What the reader needs to understand is that the contradiction is what fuels any movement of energy, life would not be possible otherwise.

---

[27] Abstract for the 2nd chapter in Adrian Mirel Petrariu's thesis on *Levels of Reality in Social Systems*, Bucharest, 2013.

In what will follow, we shall see some of the most common contradictions we are facing in everyday life. These have been named alignments by Adrian Mirel Petrariu, Ph. D. in his works and each of them is an isomorphic contextualization of the general Cosmos – Chaos contradiction.

> The universe is constructed of tension between order and disorder, between cosmos and chaos, between law and opportunities, between organization and entropy, between information and uncertainty, between objective and subjective.[28]

What the Transdisciplinary Coach needs "to do" is to make the client see the existent contradiction. Because, in order for the logic of the included third to be applied, the tension produced by the contradiction needs to be maximum supported by system in which the contradiction exists.

If the tension does not reach maximum, the contradiction will dissolve, and the included third will not appear.

In either case, the energy will *move*, up or down, as it is not possible not to. If the path of effort and tension is not taken, the only possible path is that of least resistance.

Learning how to see the two poles of a contradiction and learning how to live with the emotional tension in order to better understand the situation is a transdisciplinary action.

---

[28] Adrian Mirel Petrariu, *Levels of Reality in Social Systems*, Bucharest, 2012, page 28.

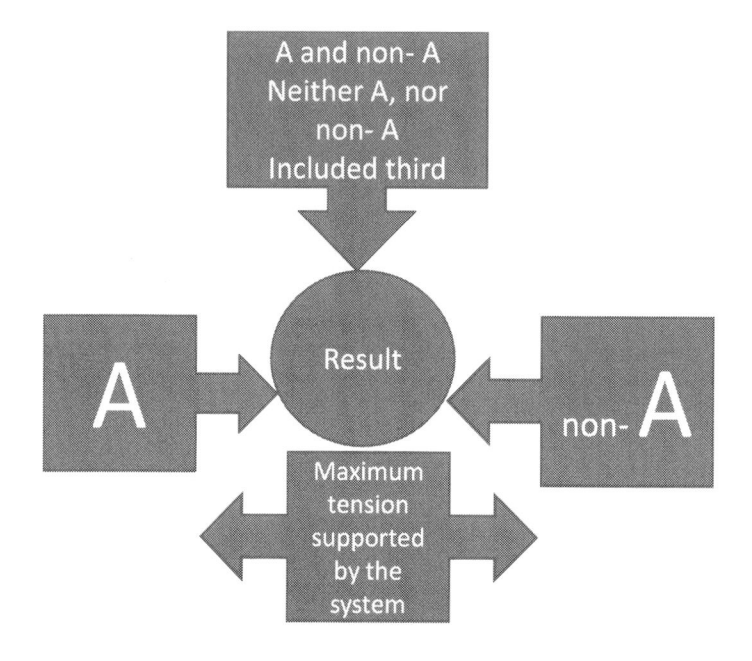

The above illustration[29] shows the described situation.

In either case, the energy will *move*, up or down, as it is not possible not to. If the path of effort and tension is not taken, the only possible path is that of least resistance.

If we go down, from this point of view, we will reach an immediate state of Calm. If we try to go up, that is to live the tension, we will get to the included third.

---

[29] Adrian Mirel Petrariu, *Levels of Reality in Social Systems*, Bucharest, 2012, page 26.

Alignments

Starting with the contradiction between Chaos and Cosmos, we will have some basic contradictions in everyday life, which are to be found in the next illustration[30]. The list is growing.

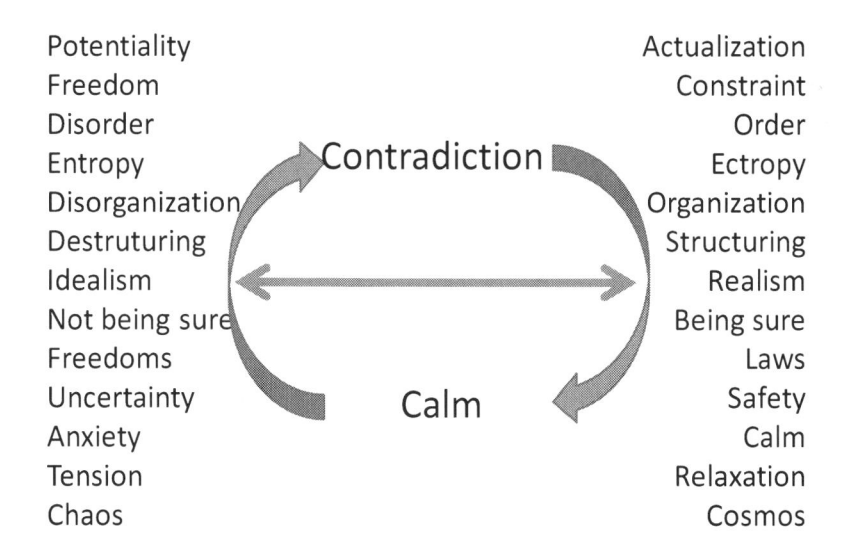

Potentiality		Actualization
Freedom		Constraint
Disorder		Order
Entropy	**Contradiction**	Ectropy
Disorganization		Organization
Destruturing		Structuring
Idealism	⟷	Realism
Not being sure		Being sure
Freedoms		Laws
Uncertainty	**Calm**	Safety
Anxiety		Calm
Tension		Relaxation
Chaos		Cosmos

Unity, Complexity, Simple-ness

We live in a world that becomes more and more complex each day. Numerous disciplines and factors to be observed, rules and regulations. It has been like this since the beginning of the world, and

---

[30] Adrian Mirel Petrariu, *The Mythology of the Energy*: Transdisciplinarity, the Force of Gurdjieff and the Tarot, Magisteria, 2015, page 312.

through tradition and religion man has tried to gain unity. If not in the outside world, at least in the inside world of the soul.

However, the contradiction between Unity and Complexity sometimes has an easy solution, by reconciling it in Simple-ness.

Complex problems have simple solutions and it is always simpler to understand one thing (unity) than a lot of things.

If we consider the different levels of reality, a complex problem from one level of reality can have a simple solution in another level of reality. Business sector problems can have solutions in the Life sector, and the other way around. Unsolved issues in the Life sector can generate problems in dealing with a team of professionals in the Business sector, and a burning issue in the Business team can generate tension in the personal level.

Status

Developed by Keith Johnstone, the improvisational theatre master, the Status concept is quite easy to grasp, but sometimes invisible in the everyday life: we have high status and low status, and whenever two people have the same status, a conflict will appear.

As a general representative of high status, one can think of Clint Eastwood. As a low status representative, Woody Allen.

Both type of statuses have advantages, and can be used to achieve a goal or manipulate others.

And life anything else in the universe, there are different degrees in each of the status: if two people have the same status, let's say a low one, a conflict can be avoided if one of them lowers the status even more.

A key note is required here: the status does not actually depend on the social position of the person. The easiest example is with the general who has high status in front of the soldiers, and low status in front of his wife.

This social contradiction of status that lies beyond the gender and position can be reconciled only by having a specific aim.

The Six Processes

One of the most interesting applications is that of the six processes in nature, life or business. Developed by J. G. Bennett[31], this concept is starting to be applied and used in many situations.

In what will follow, the six basic contradictions in the universe will be presented.

> The greatest exterior contradictions in the Universe are therefore: liberty- constraint (laws of movement and potentialization-actualization), immortality-efemerity (specialization and necessity of structuration and destructuration of the energy) and perfection-imperfection (optimization of the perpetual movement).[32]

---

[31] J. G. Bennett, *The Dramatic Universe*, Claymont Communications, 1987, page 102.
[32] Adrian Mirel Petrariu, *The Mythology of the Energy*: Transdisciplinarity, the Force of Gurdjieff and the Tarot, Magisteria, 2015, page 297.

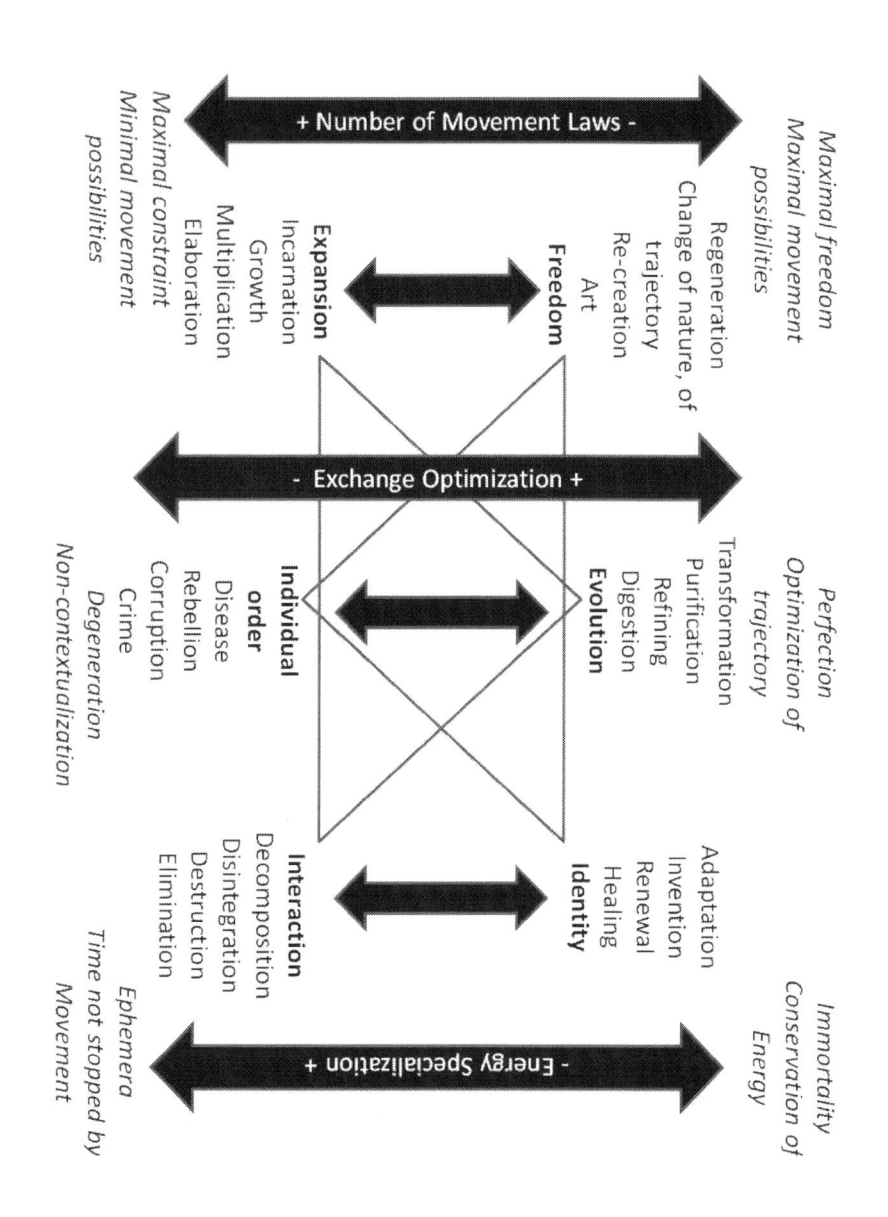

Transdisciplinary Coaching, Vol. 1

I see Relationships

The third installment of the transdisciplinary methodology in coaching is to see the relationships between the different aspects of a situation.

As everything is connected to everything else, in a beautiful interdependence, intelligence is sometimes measured by the number of connections one sees between the same things and not by enlarging the number of things.

A basic rule is to pay attention to the fact that when a change of level is present, inversion – like in a mirror – is to be applied.

When looking at types of relationships, we should have in mind the fact that no closed system can live long enough, and exchanges are necessary in order to maintain life. In other words, relationships are a way of feeding and there is a correct[33] way of doing this and an incorrect way. From this point of view, everybody feeds on everybody.

Masculine and Feminine

One of the most important types of relationships is that between a man and a woman, or between masculine and feminine, which is a polarization between (+) and (-).

Masculine sexuality is about adding; feminine sexuality is about subtracting – and the clothing styles are proof of this.

---

[33] When having a certain aim. There is no "right" or "wrong" without a goal to be referenced to.

Masculine sexuality is about filling something else, while feminine sexuality is about being filled – and the form of the sexual organs are a proof of this.

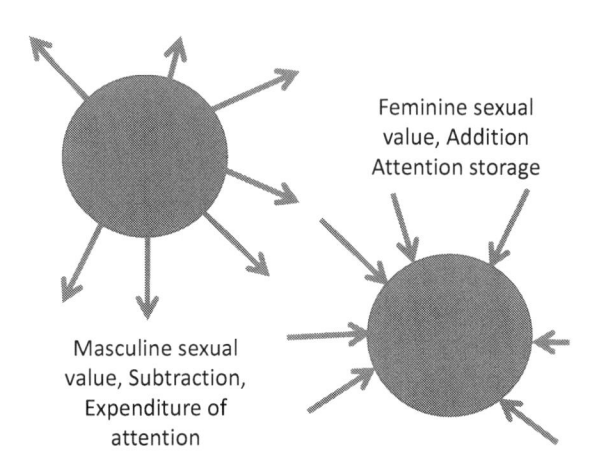

Feminine sexual value, Addition Attention storage

Masculine sexual value, Subtraction, Expenditure of attention

These being said, there are a few simple consequences[34] that need to be observed when relating to this aspect:

- an equal (+) and a (-) will easily have a relationship because of the conservation of energy through optimization of expenditure.
- a powerful (+) will have the tendency to fill the biggest (-); will also have an issue with a bigger (-) because of the insatisfaction of completely filling it.
- a (-) will have the tendency to search for the biggest (+) available in order to be filled by it.

---

[34] Adrian Mirel Petrariu, *The Mythology of the Energy*: Transdisciplinarity, the Force of Gurdjieff and the Tarot, Magisteria, 2015, page 333.

- a (+) will think like a (+) while a (-) will think like a (-).

If we have these things in mind, we will see a lot of situations where the above consequences will apply, regardless of the natural sex of the persons involved, like that of an employer (-) that needs to hire an employee (+): the employer will want to have the best possible employee for that particular job, even if the payment is not the best; two equal companies will tend to start partnerships; etc.

The Dramatic Triangle

It is with great pleasure that I will introduce here a very good tool to be used in seeing relationships: the dramatic triangle of Stephen Karpman, M.D.

Student of Eric Berne, he stated that the three roles of Victim, Persecutor and Rescuer are in a close relationship.

In order to understand this better, let's see more details[35] about each of the roles:

---

[35] http://aawa.co/blog/karpmans-drama-triangle/

Karpman's Drama Triangle

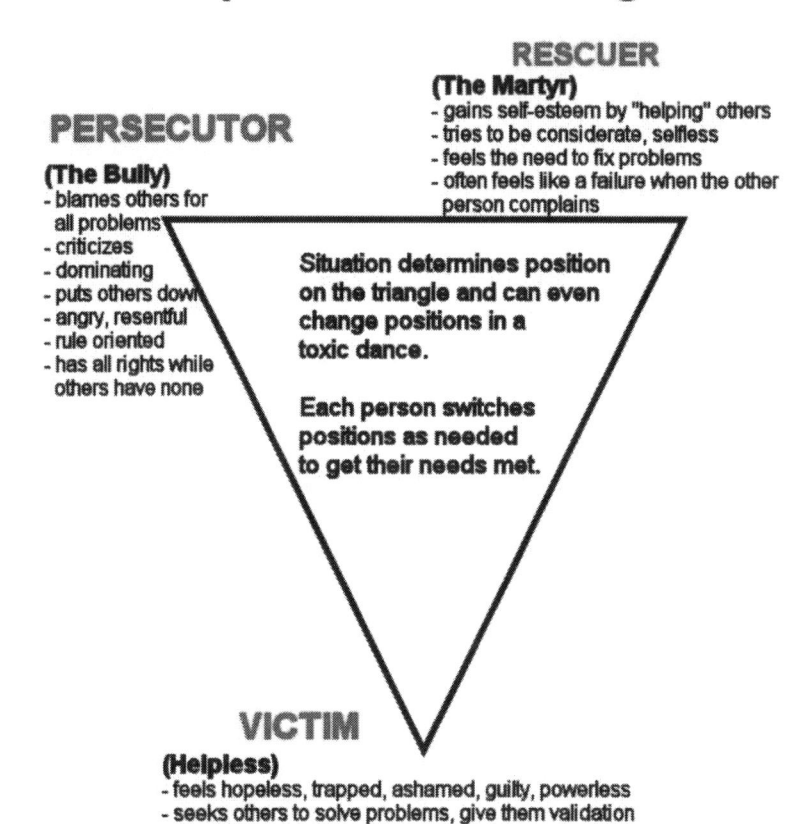

PERSECUTOR
(The Bully)
- blames others for all problems
- criticizes
- dominating
- puts others down
- angry, resentful
- rule oriented
- has all rights while others have none

RESCUER
(The Martyr)
- gains self-esteem by "helping" others
- tries to be considerate, selfless
- feels the need to fix problems
- often feels like a failure when the other person complains

Situation determines position on the triangle and can even change positions in a toxic dance.

Each person switches positions as needed to get their needs met.

VICTIM
(Helpless)
- feels hopeless, trapped, ashamed, guilty, powerless
- seeks others to solve problems, give them validation
- refuses to make decisions, solve problem, or seek professional help
- dependent

The change can be from falling to horizontal, or to vertical – ascending.

The horizontal positioning requires a functional triangle:

Tarot

One profound way to intervene in the Drama Triangle is for family members to learn not to rescue each other. The other is to stop allowing others to rescue you.[36]

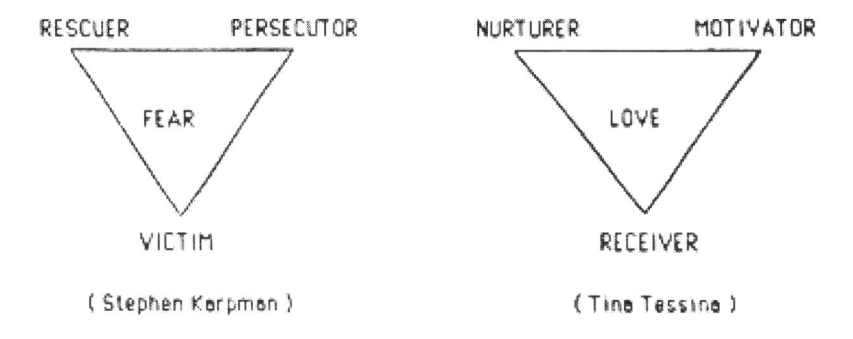

```
RESCUER      PERSECUTOR        NURTURER     MOTIVATOR
   \            /                 \            /
    \   FEAR   /                   \   LOVE   /
     \        /                     \        /
      \      /                       \      /
       VICTIM                         RECEIVER

   ( Stephen Karpman )            ( Tina Tessina )
```

The verticality[37] can be pursued as follows:
- The Victim is a person that has possibilities of movement, which can be used in various ways.
- The Rescuer is an observer that can leave the reality to exist.
- The Persecutor can just as easily protect.

---

[36] http://www.tinatessina.com/avoiding-the-drama-triangle.html
[37] Most probably, Alain Cardon.

Obedience

The universe is a big open system and requires interdependence of all its components. As such, it is relevant to know when and to whom one must give obedience.

As the law of contradiction applies here as well, we will have submission by love or by fear, with different results[38] in each case.

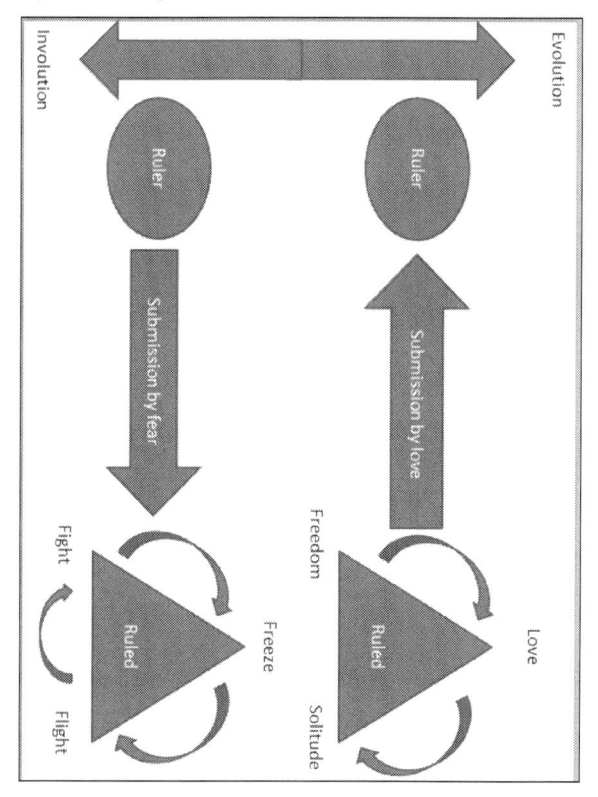

---
[38] Adrian Mirel Petrariu, *On Emotions*, Magisteria, 2017, page 71.

As Adrian Mirel Petrariu posits[39]:

> The third thing is the love for existence. I will obey you, or you obey me, or we will obey each other, because we both love the things we make together.
>
> Well, this is how a poisonous relation can go upwards. But this thing implies accepting the other's person freedom – which is a very difficult thing; it also means accepting the other's solitude – which is even harder.

Team Coaching

Bearing in mind that a team is composed of people, and moreover people with different degrees of responsibility, the Transdisciplinary approach would be to address the team leader, the team as a whole and each person in the team separately.

This approach[40] has been offered before on the market with success.

Also, it is important to never forget that any whole is bigger than the sum of its parts and special attention should be given to the transition between the different levels of reality that are governed by different laws.

---

[39] Adrian Mirel Petrariu, *On Emotions*, Magisteria, 2017, page 73.
[40] http://burwellventures.com/team-coaching/

team coaching r3sults

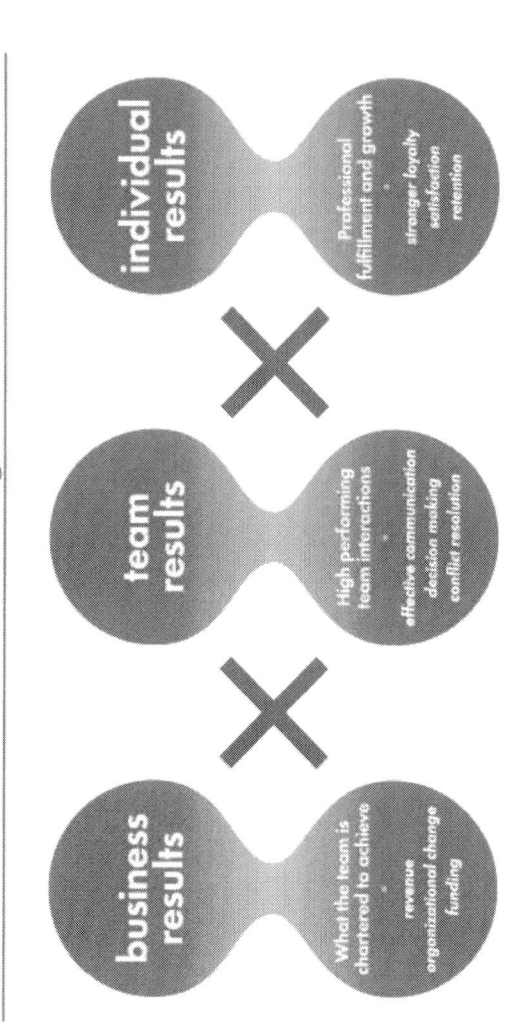

individual results
Professional fulfillment and growth
- stronger loyalty
- satisfaction
- retention

×

team results
High performing team interactions
- effective communication
- decision making
- conflict resolution

×

business results
What the team is chartered to achieve
- revenue
- organizational change
- funding

Tarot

What's with the Tarot?

Since the dawn of time man has used symbols to describe reality and to communicate about the reality. The cards from the Tarot de Marseille are no exception to this: 22 cards – similar to Renaissance paintings – have been transmitted from generation to generation.

Although the majority of people consider their use is for fortune telling – while some people actually use the Tarot cards this way – their true purpose is to transmit a certain type of knowledge through the use of symbols, just like a book, or a mathematical formula.

In this book we shall use them precisely so: in order to illustrate a situation and moreover in a transdisciplinary manner: to see the different levels of reality, the contradictions and the interdependence. Needless to say, this is the only book in the world that uses the Tarot cards in this manner.[41]

Short History

The history of the Tarot cards is vague. They appeared in 15th century in Europe and were used to play cards, just like a regular pack of cards. Since 18th century, the use for divination emerged and spread throughout the world.

---

[41] With one exception: Adrian Mirel Petrariu, *The Mythology of the Energy: Transdisciplinarity, the Force of Gurdjieff and the Tarot*, Magisteria, 2015.

The first documented tarot packs were recorded between 1430 and 1450 in Milan, Ferrara and Bologna when additional trump cards with allegorical illustrations were added to the common four-suit pack. These new decks were called carte da trionfi, triumph cards, and the additional cards known simply as trionfi, which became "trumps" in English. These cards are documented in a written statement in the court records in Florence, in 1440.[42]

There are some old variations of the pictures in the cards, but the most important one – used in this book also – is the one called Tarot de Marseille. In the recent years, numerous variations of the redrawing of the cards are available, like the Egyptian Tarot, the Magician's Tarot, etc. But none of these have the knowledge transmitted by the Tarot de Marseille.

The Tarot Deck

The cards are divided between Major Arcana and Minor Arcana.

The Major Arcana, the greater secrets, 22 cards, are what we shall use in this book. Each of them – with one exception – has a number, and each of them – with one exception – has a name.

---

[42] https://en.wikipedia.org/wiki/Tarot

The Minor Arcana, the lesser secrets, 56 cards, in four sets, like the usual pack of cards, with simpler symbols, we will not use in this book. They are divided into four suits of 14 cards each; 10 numbered cards and 4 court cards: King, Queen, Knight and Page/Jack, in each of the four tarot suits.

The Marseilles' numbered minor arcana cards do not have scenes depicted on them; rather, they sport a geometric arrangement of the number of suit symbols (e.g., swords, rods/wands, cups, coins/pentacles) corresponding to the number of the card (accompanied by botanical and other non-scenic flourishes), while the court cards are often illustrated with flat, two-dimensional drawings.[43]

Knowledge by Numbers

Numerology has always played an important part both in sciences and in spiritual disciples such as astrology. In this book, however, we will not use the common interpretations of each number from 1 to 9, but we will try to keep an eye for relationships between different cards based not only on their similar appearance but on their numeric components also – how many people in the card, for example.

---

[43] https://en.wikipedia.org/wiki/Tarot

The Major Arcana

In what will follow, I shall present each of the 22 cards in the Major Arcana and give a basic explanation for the card and its symbols. This explanation should be just like a starting point in the understanding associated with the particular card and with its use in the Transdisciplinary Coaching.

In many of the cards, the action depicted in the image gives an important clue as to the meaning of the card, in the most basic sense.

The name of the card, originally in French, is also quite important, as it represents, in some cases, an included third. This means, that by translating the name in other language, some meaning will be lost. However, I shall give the usual English translations as well.

The reader should get acquainted with the name, the number, the picture and the meaning of each card and try to use the available personal experience in order to have a real understanding.

Le Mat

Number: It is the only card without a number.

Name: The Fool. The Buffoon.

General: Freedom of movement. Essence. Looking to the future. Madness. Creative urge. Irrational.

Coaching: The energy.
Detachment vs. Ignorance.
Two possible ways of ignoring a contradiction.
The psychic type of matter (out of the four types of matter – physical, biological, affective, psychic).

Relationships: Same posture and position as the card no. 13. The position of the stick is identical also.

LE · MAT

Le Bateleur

Number: 1.

Name: The Magician. The Juggler. Trickster (sacred).

General: Dexterity. Talent. Showmanship. Charisma.

Coaching: The physical center of man (instinctive and motor systems).
Physical action in the world.

Relationships: Similar hat with The Force.
Similar wand with The World.

LE·BATELEUR

La Papesse

Number: 2.

Name: The High Priestess.

General: Gestation. Accumulation. Faith. Coldness.

Coaching: The (lower) emotional center of man.
Positive and negative emotions.
Observing the rules.
Stiffness based on experience of the past.

Relationships: Similar crown with The Pope.

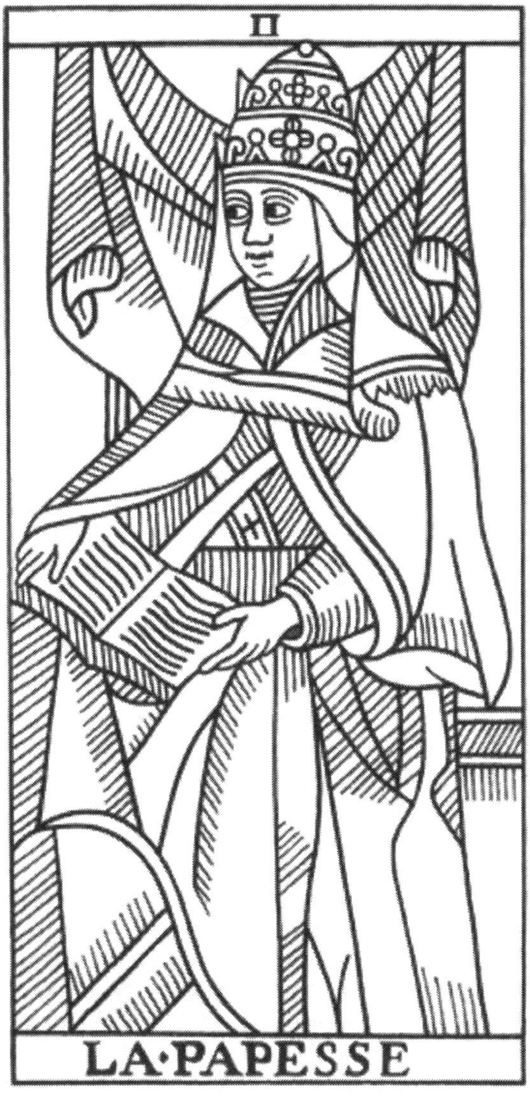
II
LA·PAPESSE

L'Impératrice

Number: 3.

Name: The Empress.

General: Creativity. Abundance. Ferment.

Coaching: The (lower) intellectual center of man.
Verbal logic (dictionary logic) and formal logic (based on experiences).
Binary logic most of the time.

Relationships: Similar eagle and scepter with The Emperor.
Similar position with The Justice.

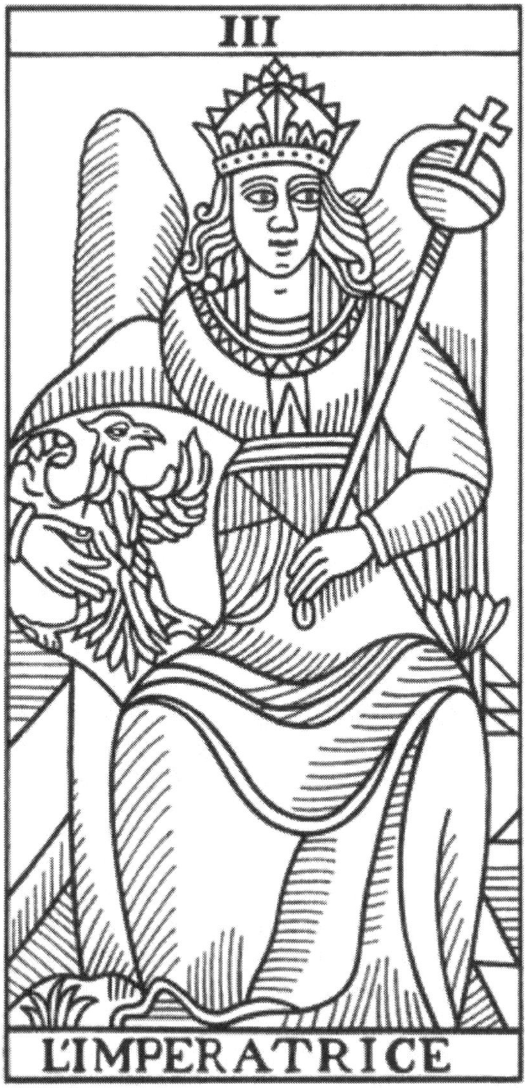
III
L'IMPERATRICE

L'Empereur

Number: 4.

Name: The Emperor.

General: Stability. Authority. Rational mind. Patriarchy. Power.

Coaching: The higher intellectual center of man.
Consciousness.
Objective logic. Ternary logic.

Relationships: Similar eagle and scepter with The Empress.

L'EMPEREUR

Le Pape

Number: 5.

Name: The Pope.

General: Verticality. Mediator. Communication. Dogma.

Coaching: The (higher) emotional center of man.
Real feelings (love, faith, hope).
Individuality.
Building bridges.
Connecting businesses.

Relationships: Similar card with The Sun and The Devil, and The Chariot: one big figure and two small figures.

Tarot

L'Amoureux

Number: 6.

Name: The Lover.

General: Choice. Conflict. Social life. Unconditional love.

Coaching: The (higher) physical center of man (sexual).
Real Will.
Pure action.
Waiting for a higher decision to be made.
Separating business from pleasure.

Relationships: Similar card with The Judgment: one angel and three humans.

Tarot

Le Chariot

Number: 7.

Name: The Chariot.

General: Travel. Domination. Action in the world. Triumph.

Coaching: The internal structure of man: physical part (the chariot), affective part (the horses), and intellectual part (the driver).
Correct order of action (intellect -> emotion -> body).
Action based on experience of the past.
Business protocol.

Relationships: Similar card with The Pope, The Sun and The Devil: one big figure and two small figures.

Tarot

La Justice

Number: 8.

Name: The Justice.

General: Balance. Valor. Trial.

Coaching: When something goes up, something else is going down.
Ternary state of balance (the need for three elements in order to reach a state of balance, not two – the hand and the balance).
Legal matters.

Relationships: Similar position with The Empress.
Similar background with The Pope (columns).

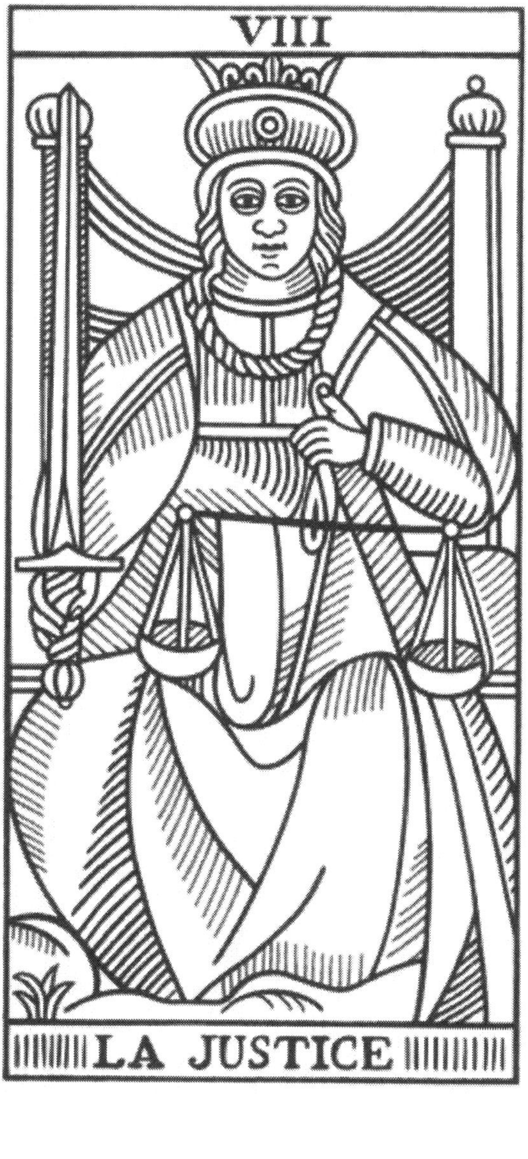
VIII
LA JUSTICE

L'Ermite

Number: 9.

Name: The Hermit.

General: Crisis. Therapy. Passage. Wisdom. Ascetic. Walking backwards.

Coaching: Energy to understand the world in which we live in.
The ternary that leads to Understanding: observation (the eyes), information (the lantern) and verification (the stick).
Advice from the elders.

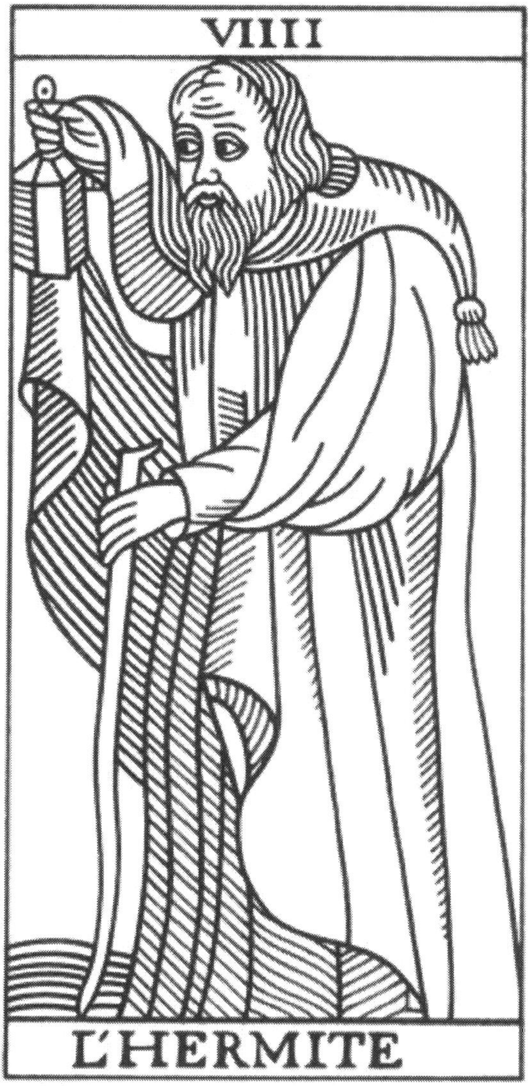
VIIII
L'HERMITE

La Roue de Fortune

Number: 10.

Name: The Wheel of Fortune.

General: Luck. Cycle. Fate. Blockage.

Coaching: Beginning of the social level in the cards.
Eternal change between Chaos and Cosmos.
Strategic advantage.
The law of accident.

Tarot

LA·ROVE·DE·FORTVNE

La Force

Number: 11.

Name: The Strength.

General: Forcing. New beginning Anger. Creativity.

Coaching: Emotional dominance as an antidote of the physical force; and vice-versa.
Using leverage as means for action.
Empowering a woman for a man's job.

Relationships: Similar hat with The Magician.

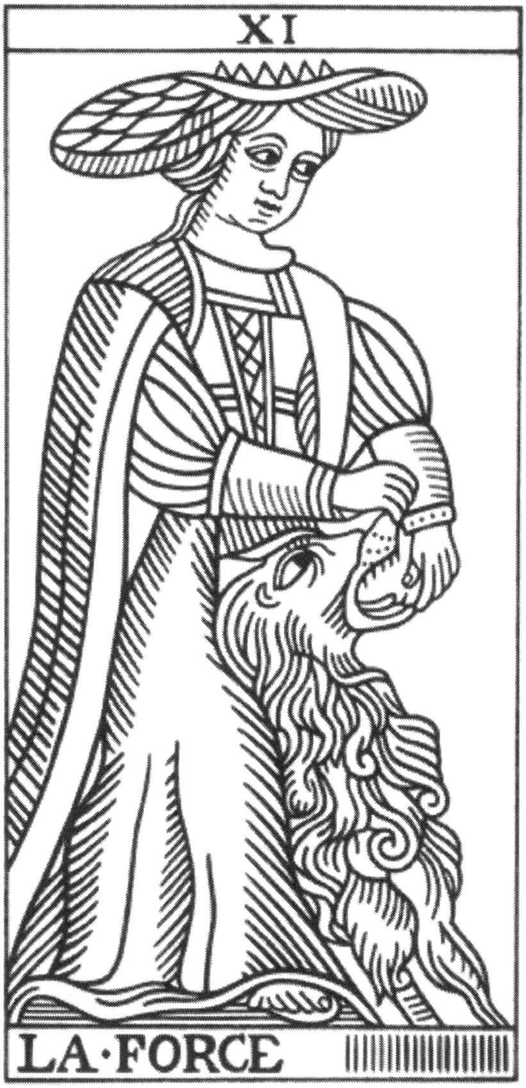
XI
LA·FORCE

Le Pendu

Number: 12.

Name: The Hanged Man.

General: Self-sacrifice. Meditation. Halt. Waiting.

Coaching: Changing the perspective. Illumination.
The inversion that takes place when passing from one level to another.
Debts from the past that are an obstacle to development.

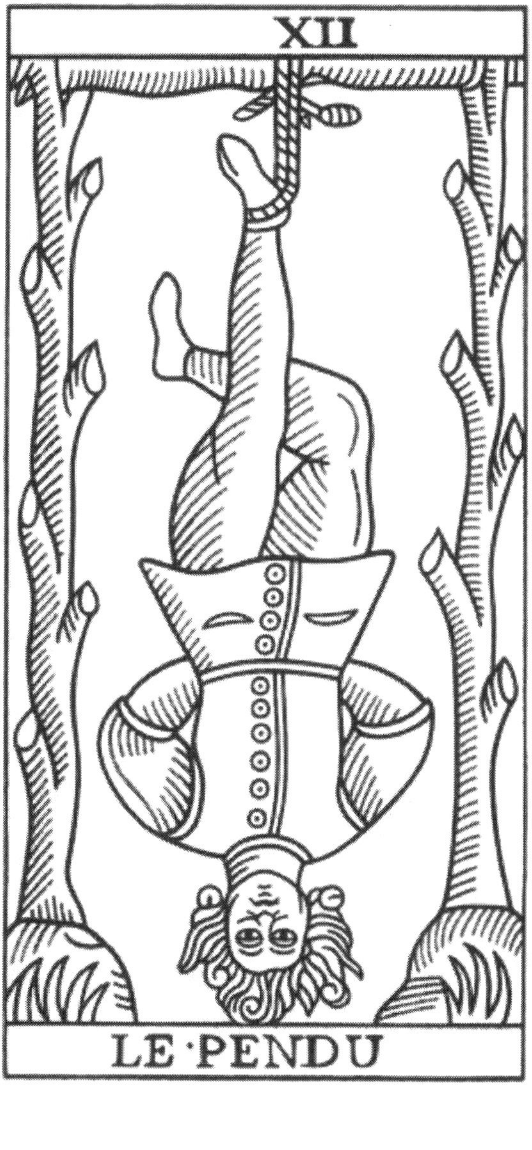
XII
LE·PENDU

Sin Nom

Number: 13.

Name: There is no name on this card.

General: Mutation. Cleansing. Harvest. Revolution. Transformation.

Coaching: Absence.
Re-birth. Death.
Separation in order to succeed. "Divide et impera."
The end of an old business.
"There will be blood."

Relationships: Similar posture and position with The Fool.

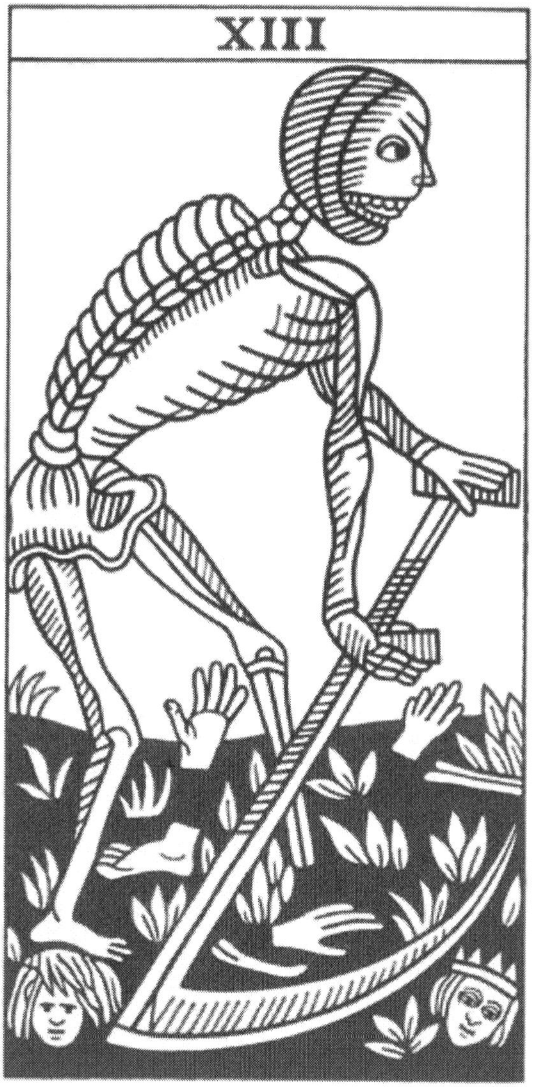
XIII

Tempérance

Number: 14.

Name: Temperance.

General: Guardian angel. Healing. Health.

Coaching: Objective view about a situation.
Seeing the beginning and the end of an object/ situation.
Going around the bush; hesitation.
Doing the same business cycle again and again.

Relationships: Similar vases with The Star.

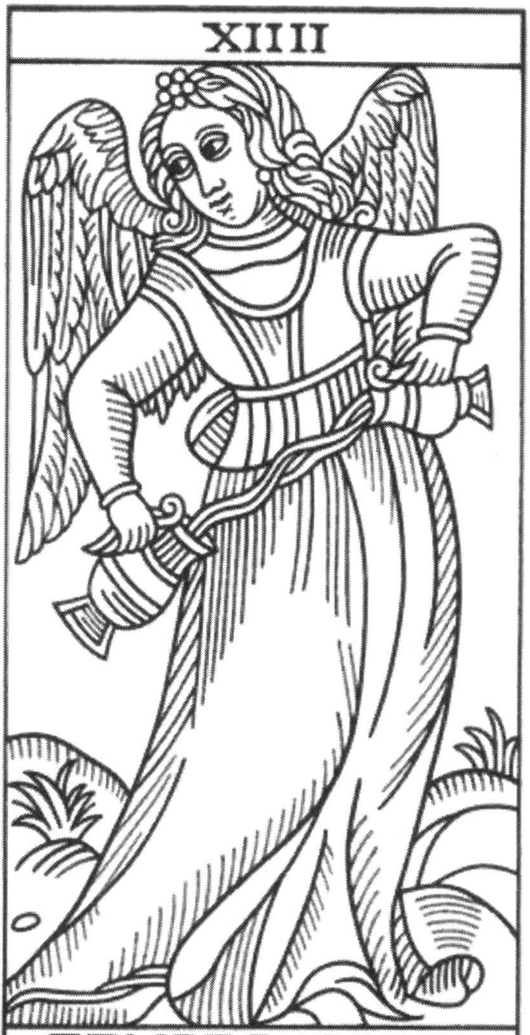
XIIII
TEMPERANCE

Le Diable

Number: 15.

Name: The Devil.

General: Attachments. Temptation. Passions. Sexuality. Subconscious.

Coaching: The Devil.
Social attachments.
Money.
Corporate bounds.

Relationships: Similar card with The Sun, The Pope and The Chariot: one big figure and two small figures.

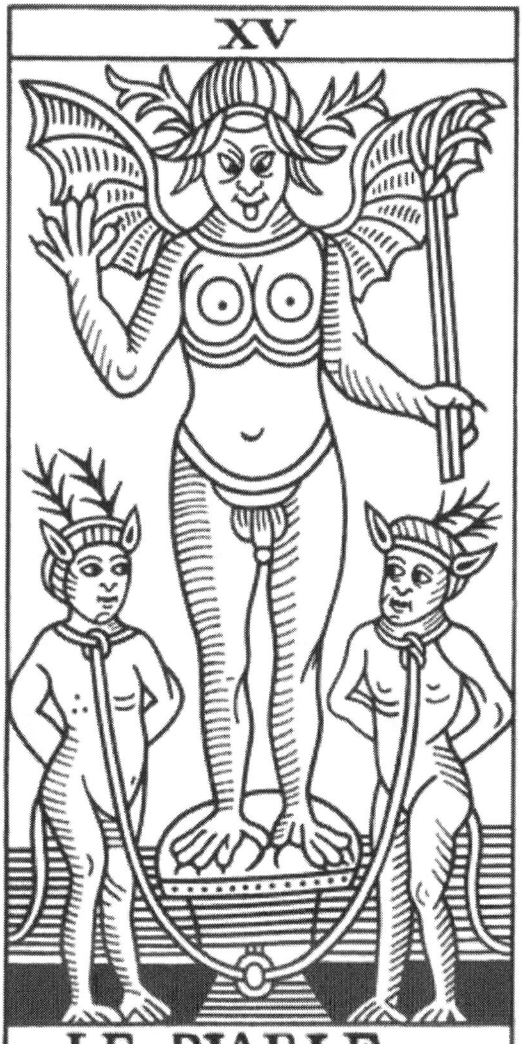
XV
LE • DIABLE

La Maison Dieu

Number: 16.

Name: The Tower. House of God. The House/ God.

General: Body. Divine. Shock. Exploding. Fortunate change of situation.

Coaching: Construction and deconstruction.
The law of Falling.
Funds for a project.
Brainstorming.

Tarot

L'Étoile

Number: 17.

Name: The Star.

General: Fertility. Irrigation. To feed. Pregnancy. Purification. Generosity. Nostalgia.

Coaching: Destiny.
Degrees of freedom.
No self-calming.
Re-investing the profits.

Relationships: Similar vases with Temperance.

Tarot

La Lune

Number: 18.

Name: The Moon.

General: Intuition. Receptivity. Imagination. Madness.

Coaching: Automatic actions.
Decay of a process.
Working late shifts.
Building a business over night.

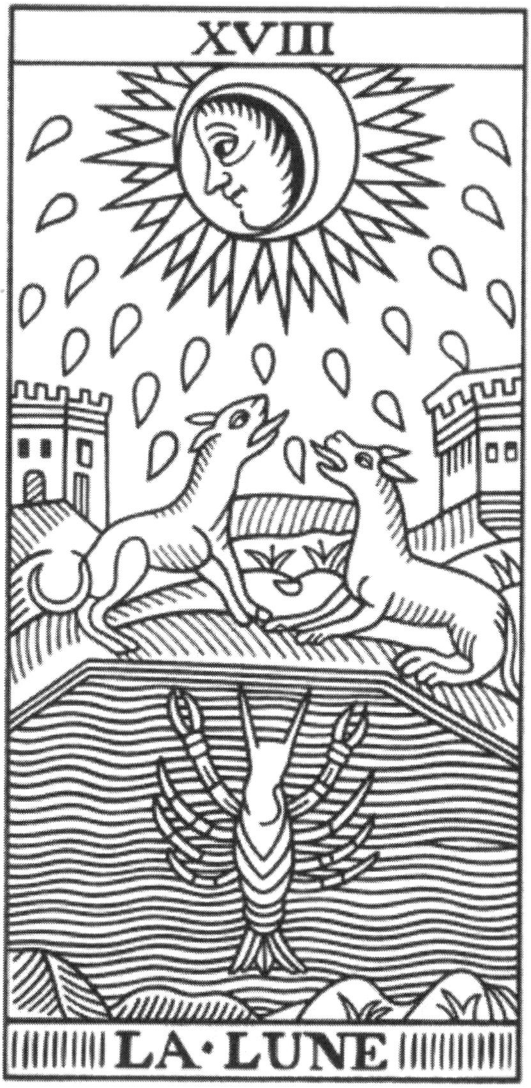
XVIII
LA·LUNE

Le Soleil

Number: 19.

Name: The Sun.

General: Twin-ship. Evolution. Rivalry. Mutual aid. New life.

Coaching: Unconditioned relationships.
Higher influences.
The biological type of matter.
Profitable alliances.
A strong foundation for a solid future.

Relationships: Similar card with The Pope, The Devil, and The Chariot: one big figure and two small figures.

Tarot

Le Jugement

Number: 20.

Name: The Judgment.

General: Birth. Vocation. Transcendence. Openness.

Coaching: Consciousness. Awakening.
Two levels of interaction.
Individual level vs. Social level.
The affective type of matter.
Paying taxes.
Retirement money.

Relationships: Similar card with The Lover: one angel and three humans.

Tarot

Le Monde

Number: 21.

Name: The World.

General: Soul. Realization. Fullness.

Coaching: The four dimensions of space.
Relationships. Interior vs. exterior.
The law of Three with its result.
The physical type of matter.
Implementing a rural business.
Surrounding yourself with capable employees.

Relationships: Similar wand with The Magician.

Tarot

Review of the Major Arcana

From the beginning until the 9th card: individual level.
From the 10th card to the 18th card: the social level.
After that, until the end: the cosmic level.

On the next page we can see all the 22 cards[44].

Big and small

Also, do observe that some of the cards have one big figure in the upper part of the card and two small figures in the lower part (like The Sun, The Pope, The Devil, etc.) All these are connected somehow.

The look

Some of the people in the cards look in a certain direction. That is, they look at some other people (in another card) or at some objects, and this creates a connection between the look and the object, between the two cards. On the next page, the Pope looks at the angel in the Lover card, for example.

---

[44] Restored version of Tarot de Marseille by Camoin & Jodorowsky.

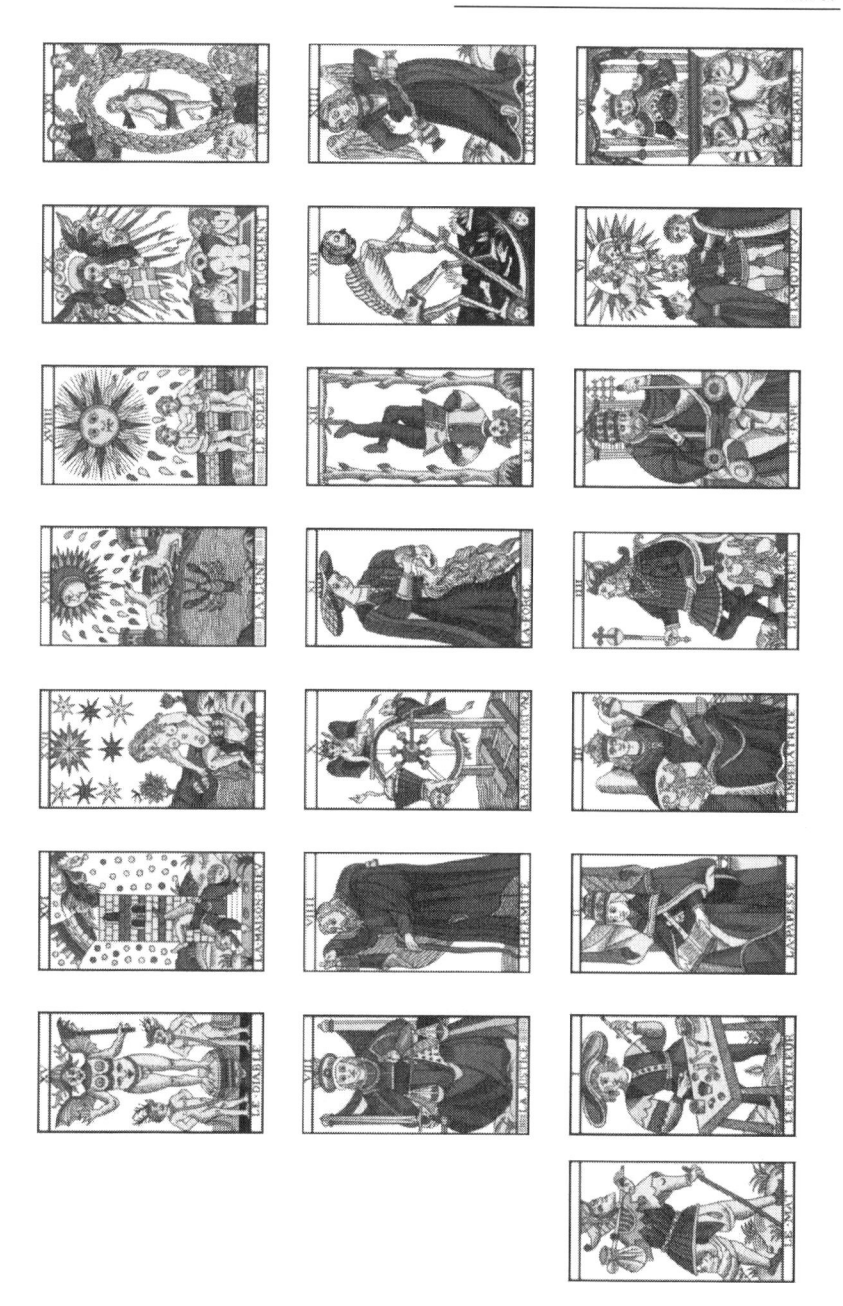

Tarot

How to Spread

Next in our voyage of Tarot comes the spread, which is a certain map that we will have when using the cards. Each map covers another point of view, another topic, like Past-Present-Future, Advantage-Disadvantage, etc.

Rules for Reading

Each time we have a Tarot client in front of us, we will have three sources of information for the reading of the cards:

1. The need/ question/ problem of the client. This should be in as much detail as possible, just like telling it to a priest or a therapist.
2. The map we choose for the reading.
3. The meanings of each card.

Based on these three sources of information, the coach will approach the client and develop the session.

Basic Spreads

Let's see some basic maps for our card reading.

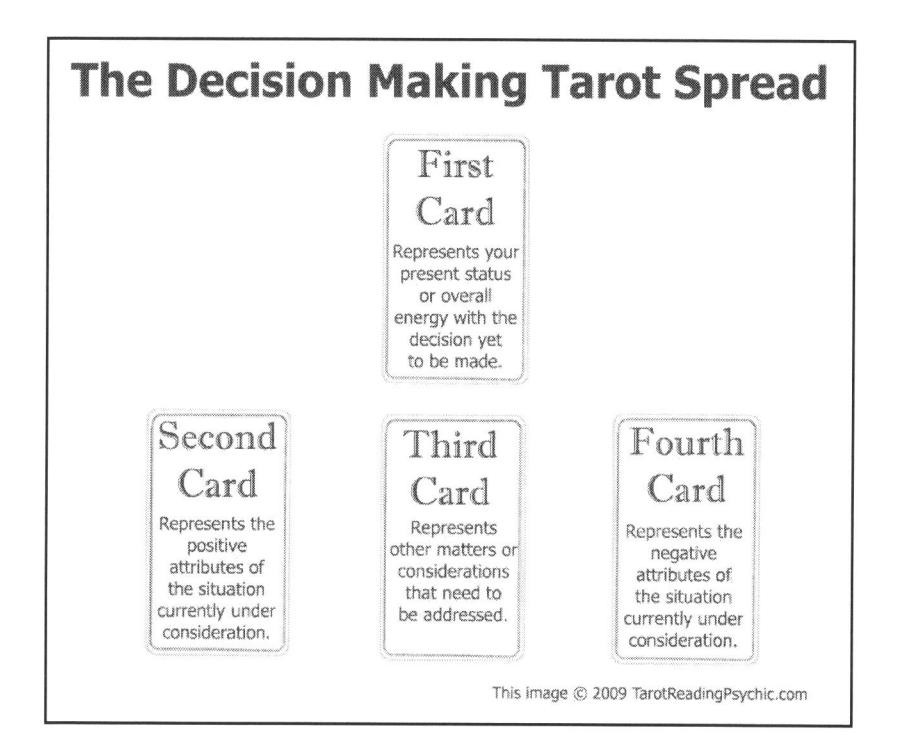

The Decision Making Tarot Spread

First Card: Represents your present status or overall energy with the decision yet to be made.

Second Card: Represents the positive attributes of the situation currently under consideration.

Third Card: Represents other matters or considerations that need to be addressed.

Fourth Card: Represents the negative attributes of the situation currently under consideration.

This image © 2009 TarotReadingPsychic.com

As we can see, the map is quite clear and we should stay with it most of the time. Even if some cards are easier to explain in different positions, we should always consider the map and the question of the client when giving the meaning.

Another simple map is as follows:

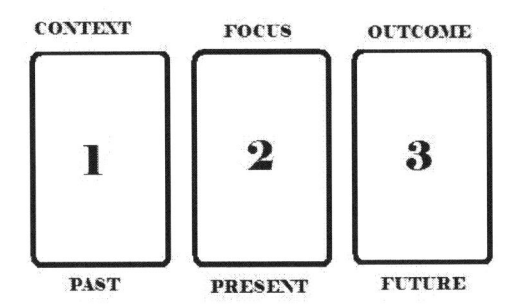

```
  CONTEXT      FOCUS      OUTCOME
 ┌───────┐  ┌───────┐  ┌───────┐
 │       │  │       │  │       │
 │   1   │  │   2   │  │   3   │
 │       │  │       │  │       │
 └───────┘  └───────┘  └───────┘
   PAST      PRESENT     FUTURE
```

Of course, even if we have a position on the map about the past, or future, we will never predict the future, just learn how to see different options and possibilities as per the client's description of the issue and the meaning of the cards.

Let's see another simple map:

The Pathway Spread

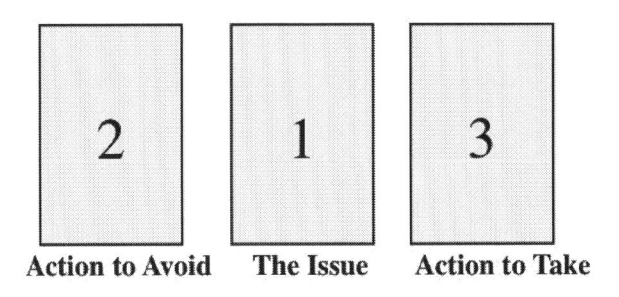

```
 ┌───────┐  ┌───────┐  ┌───────┐
 │       │  │       │  │       │
 │   2   │  │   1   │  │   3   │
 │       │  │       │  │       │
 └───────┘  └───────┘  └───────┘
Action to Avoid  The Issue  Action to Take
```

Now let's see some more complicated maps:

The Success Spread

Fourth Card
Represents the people, new ideas or things that can help you.

Second Card
Represents your current challenges and obstacles.

First Card
Represents the central issue to your question or concern.

Third Card
Represents the underlying and hidden factors that you need to be aware of.

Fifth Card
Represents the actions needed to improve your chances for success.

This image © 2009 TarotReadingPsychic.com

On the next two pages we will present the Celtic Cross spread, one of the most famous Tarot maps[45].

---
[45] A. E. Waite. The pictorial key to the Tarot: being fragments of a secret tradition under the veil of divination. W. Rider & Son, 1911.

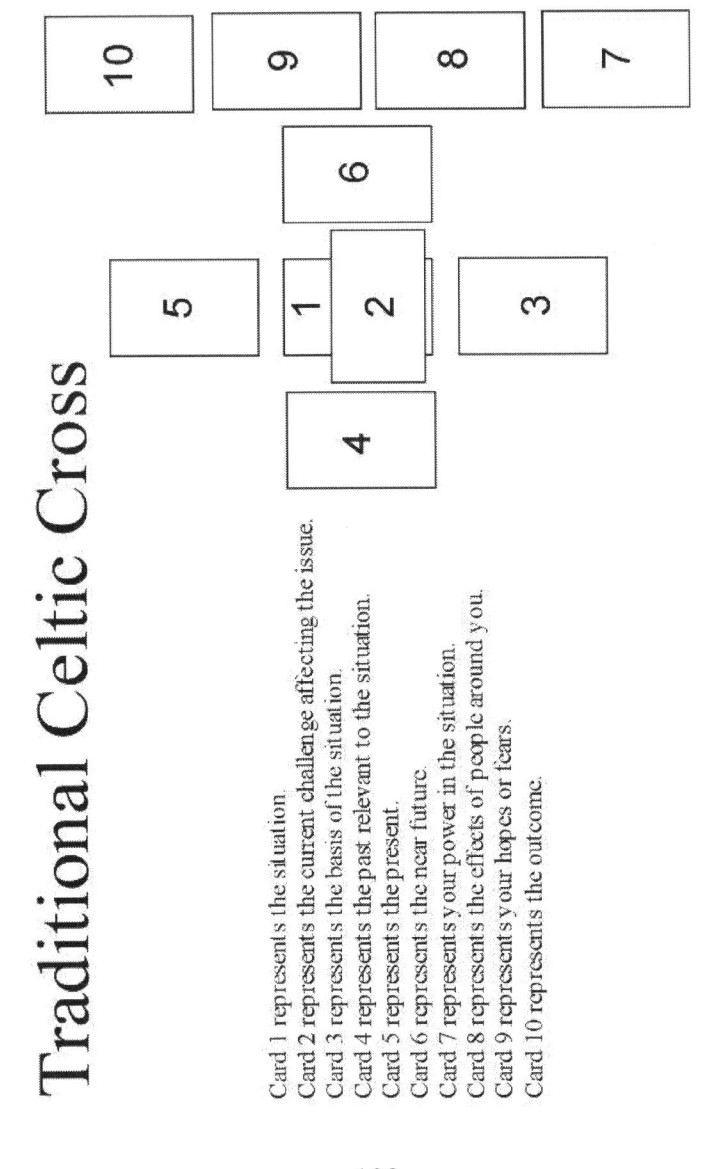

Transdisciplinary Coaching, Vol. 1

Traditional Celtic Cross

Card 1 represents the situation.
Card 2 represents the current challenge affecting the issue.
Card 3 represents the basis of the situation.
Card 4 represents the past relevant to the situation.
Card 5 represents the present.
Card 6 represents the near future.
Card 7 represents your power in the situation.
Card 8 represents the effects of people around you.
Card 9 represents your hopes or fears.
Card 10 represents the outcome.

```
        ┌───┐
        │ 3 │
        └───┘

     Significator
┌───┐   ┌═══┐    ┌───┐
│ 6 │   │ 2 │    │ 5 │
└───┘   └═══┘    └───┘
       and No. 1.

        ┌───┐
        │ 4 │
        └───┘
```

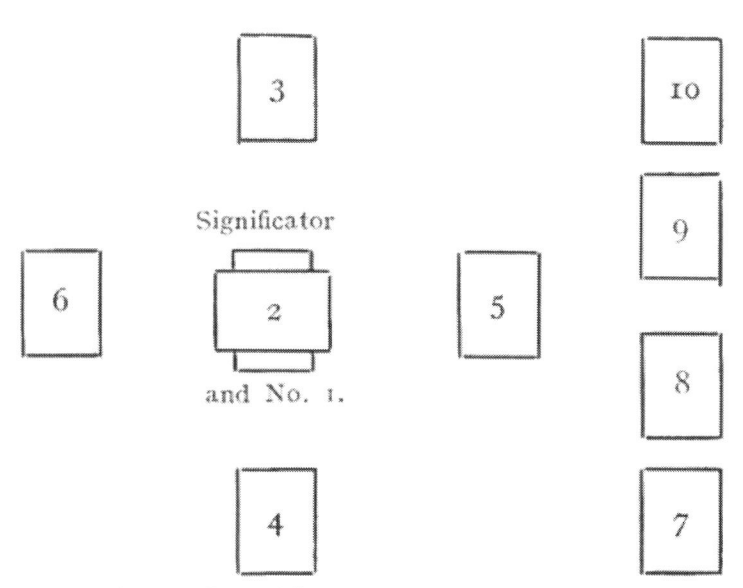

```
┌───┐
│ 10│
└───┘

┌───┐
│ 9 │
└───┘

┌───┐
│ 8 │
└───┘

┌───┐
│ 7 │
└───┘
```

{ The Significator.
{ 1. What covers him.
2. What crosses him.
3. What crowns him.
4. What is beneath him.
5. What is behind him.
6. What is before him.
7. Himself.
8. His house.
9. His hopes or fears.
10. What will come.

And let's see a map about relationships:

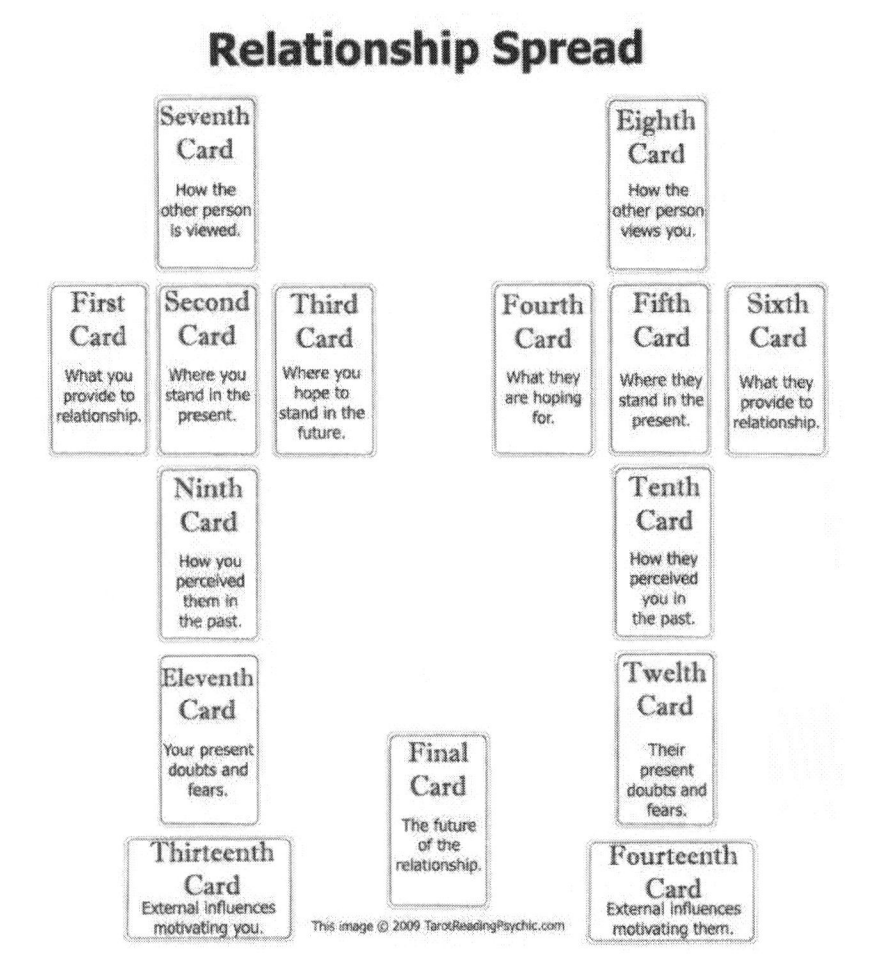

Relationship Spread

Seventh Card — How the other person is viewed.

Eighth Card — How the other person views you.

First Card — What you provide to relationship.

Second Card — Where you stand in the present.

Third Card — Where you hope to stand in the future.

Fourth Card — What they are hoping for.

Fifth Card — Where they stand in the present.

Sixth Card — What they provide to relationship.

Ninth Card — How you perceived them in the past.

Tenth Card — How they perceived you in the past.

Eleventh Card — Your present doubts and fears.

Twelfth Card — Their present doubts and fears.

Final Card — The future of the relationship.

Thirteenth Card — External influences motivating you.

Fourteenth Card — External influences motivating them.

This image © 2009 TarotReadingPsychic.com

As there is a lot of information about this subject already available on the market, we will stop here with the maps.

How to Choose

An important part of the reading process is to know which map to choose for the client's question. The client can also choose a certain map, but it is advisable that the coach will choose after listening and understanding the issue.

It is also important to pay attention at the relationship between the cards and use this in order to give meaning.

If a card "looks" in a direction that is empty, another card should be drawn and placed there for a relationship to appear.

If by any chance a card is reversed, another card should be placed above it as a solution.

Transdisciplinary Coaching with Tarot

Where to begin

After explaining the basic concepts of general coaching, transdisciplinary principles and tarot cards meaning, it's high time to understand the procedure of using tarot cards in a coaching session.

As the law of contradiction applies here as well, we will have two general situations:
- using the tarot cards in order to illustrate (the client's situation).
- using the tarot cards in order to extract meaning (the suggestions of the coach).

Illustrating the situation

As models for illustration, we will present some original examples of using the tarot cards in this manner. Most of the examples come from the fabulous works of Adrian Mirel Petrariu.

The Two Endings

There are two possible ways for a situation to end: one is for the situation not to begin (a potential that will remain a potential without becoming an actualization) and the other is for the situation to explore all its potentials by actualizing them, until no potential will remain to be actualized.

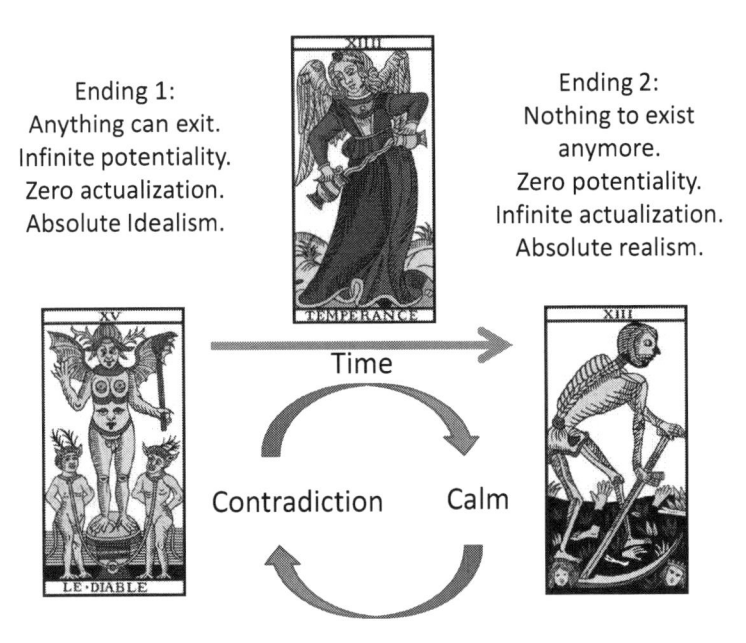

Ending 1:
Anything can exit.
Infinite potentiality.
Zero actualization.
Absolute Idealism.

Ending 2:
Nothing to exist anymore.
Zero potentiality.
Infinite actualization.
Absolute realism.

Time

Contradiction   Calm

Building bridges vs. Burning bridges

In any life or business situation, the option is there for the client to build or to destroy, mainly represented by the card House of God and by the two cards The Pope and The Devil.

Pontifex :
Building bridges

Diabolos :
Burning bridges by separation

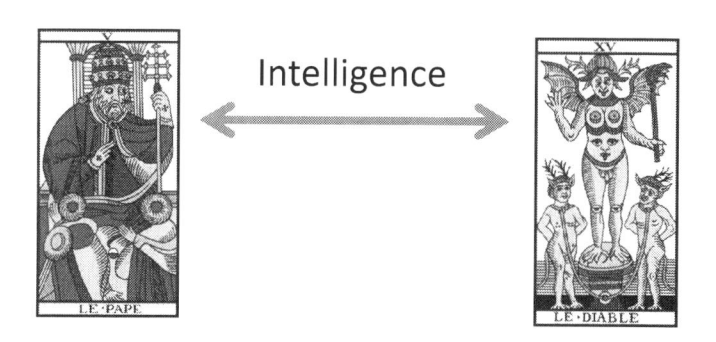

Intelligence

LE·PAPE

LE·DIABLE

The choice between the two aspects is made by intelligence, which is the ability to make relationships and connections between things one already knows.

But intelligence is always in the horizontal level, a product of binary logic, and in order to go to the next level, one needs wisdom, which is a product of ternary logic, seeing a situation in an objective manner, using symbols in order to gain meaning and formal logic.

This way, we will have the ternary between Pontifex – Diabolos – Symbolon and another ternary between Intelligence – Negligence – Wisdom, in which the first two terms of each ternary are on the horizontal, in the same level of reality.

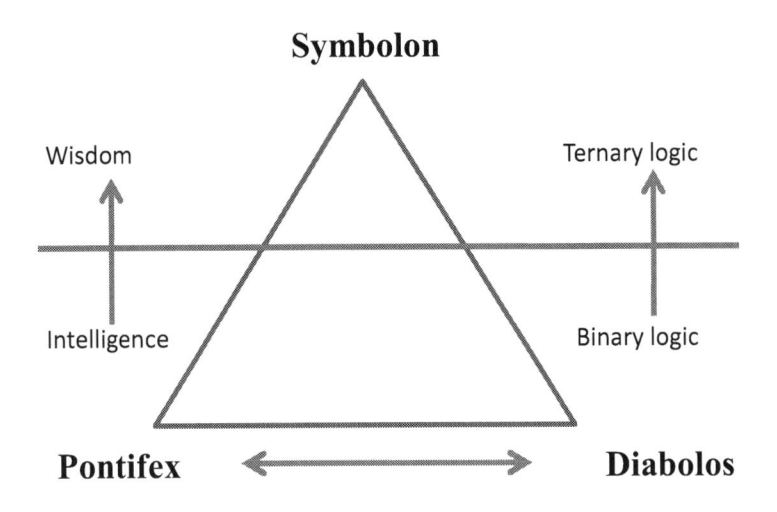

```
              Symbolon
                 /\
    Wisdom      /  \      Ternary logic
      ↑        /    \         ↑
  ━━━━━━━━━━━/━━━━━━\━━━━━━━━━━━━
      ↓      /        \        ↓
  Intelligence         Binary logic
           /_____\
   Pontifex  ←————————→  Diabolos
```

Human Map

This is a map of the human being using the octave concept derived from Gurdjieff and Orage[46] and the Tarot cards by Adrian Mirel Petrariu.

As we have already mentioned, each tarot card from 1 to 6 represents one of the human centers, while the card no. 7 represents the structure of the human being as a whole and the idea of a correct way of action for these centers.

---

[46] The Force of Gurdjieff, Vol. 3: *Oragean Version by C. Daly King*, Magisteria, 2013.

CENTER #3
Thinking
Verbal logic
Formal logic

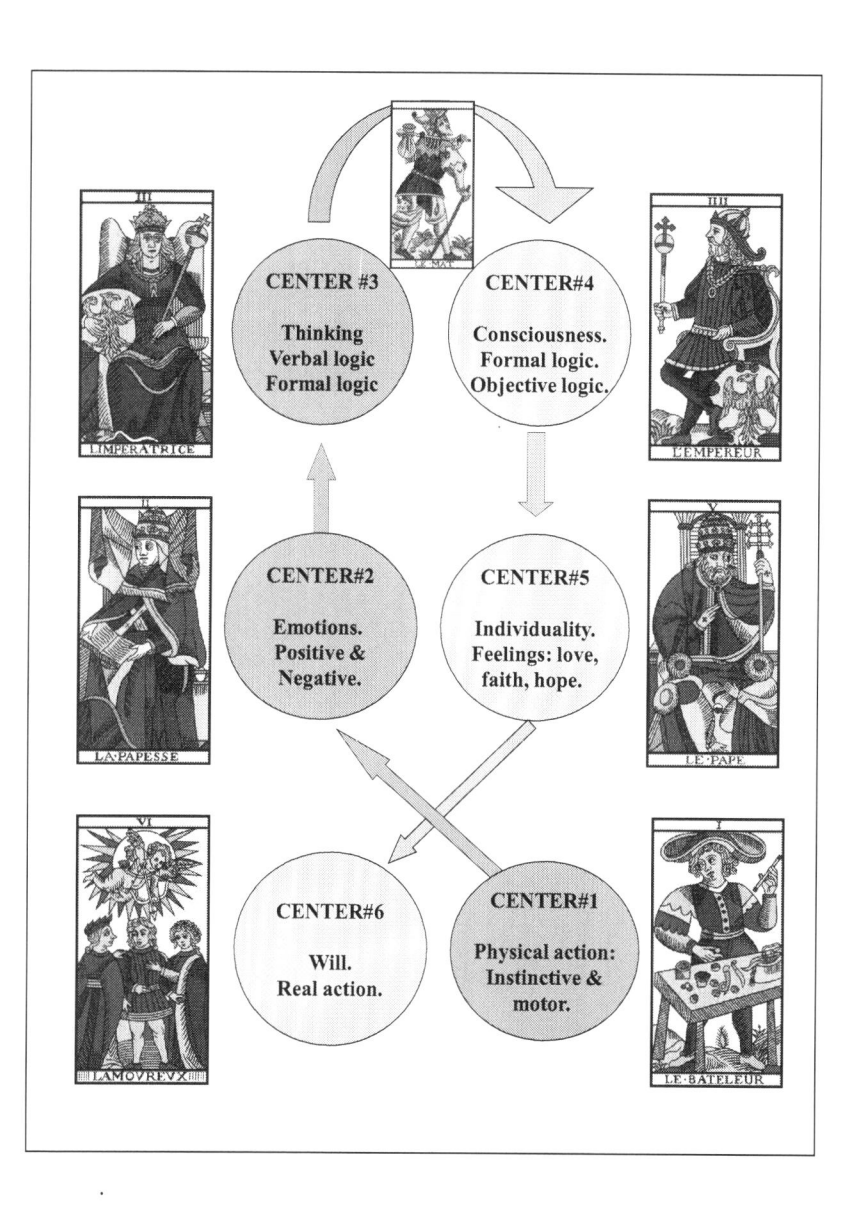

CENTER #4
Consciousness.
Formal logic.
Objective logic.

CENTER #2
Emotions.
Positive &
Negative.

CENTER #5
Individuality.
Feelings: love,
faith, hope.

CENTER #6
Will.
Real action.

CENTER #1
Physical action:
Instinctive &
motor.

The original map from Orage can be seen here. The normal connections between centers are with a straight line. The abnormal connections between center #6 and centers #1, #2 and #3 are with doble lines. The un-actualized connections with the higher centers #4, #5 and #6 are with dotted line.

For more explanations, do consult the book already mentioned.

CORTICO-PONTINE-CEREBULLAR-TRACT

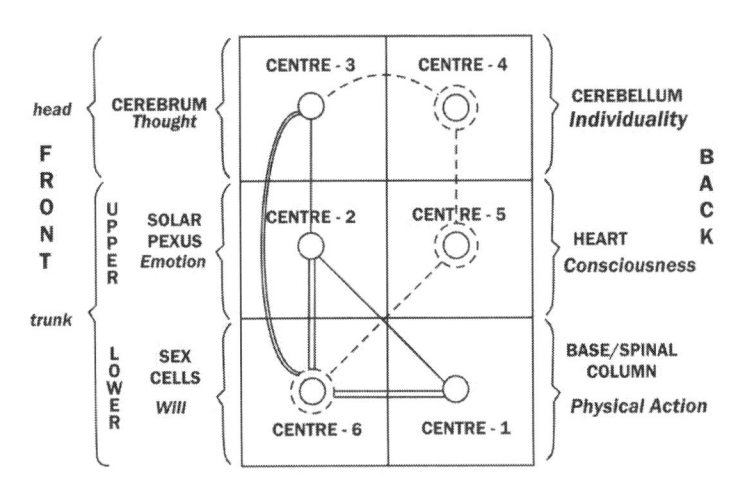

The GROW model

Here is an illustration of the famous coaching model.

Identify Objectives & Goals

Explore Options & Possibilities

Take Action, Review & Learn

Agree on Actions

The Dramatic Triangle - revisited

It is now time to see the roles in the classic Karpmann triangle in more detail[47].

The Victim can be understood like a survivor of the basic contradiction in the universe To Eat – To Be Eaten, because as we have already mentioned, we live in a universe where interdependence is the key word.

We can characterize this situation as self-calming, the lore of negative emotions where the person is unable to bear the energy of the situation and will dissipate it as quickly as possible.

The Star can be an illustration to this situation *in this case*.

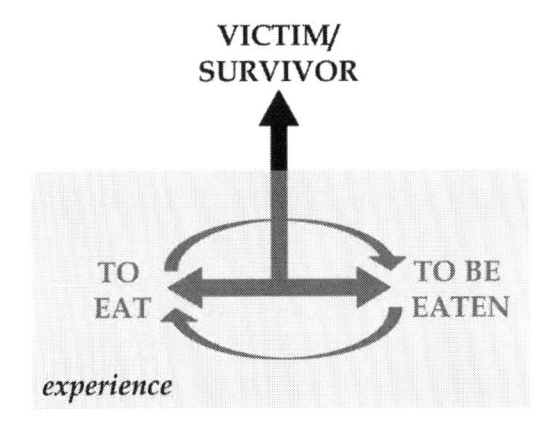

---

[47] Private workshop with Adrian Mirel Petrariu, 18th of November, 2017.

Tarot

The Persecutor is just like an attacker, a person who wants to feed on the Victim's experience, thus creating another type of circularity between the Victim and the Persecutor, a situation that can be illustrated – *in this case* – with the card Temperance.

This experience between the Victim and the Persecutor is the situation on which the Rescuer/Savior wants to feed, situation that can be illustrated by The Devil card *in this case*.

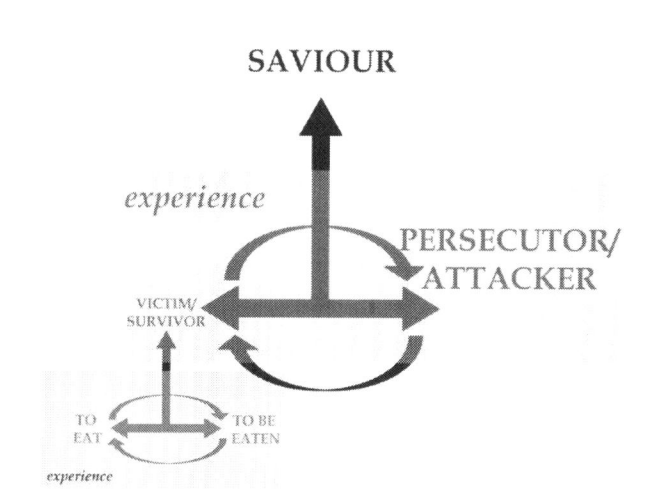

SAVIOUR

experience

PERSECUTOR/ATTACKER

VICTIM/SURVIVOR

TO EAT — TO BE EATEN

experience

We now have the classic triangle of Karpmann and we need to understand the difference between the triangle that goes down, because of self-calming and negative emotions, and the triangle that is on the horizontal, where positive emotions exist.

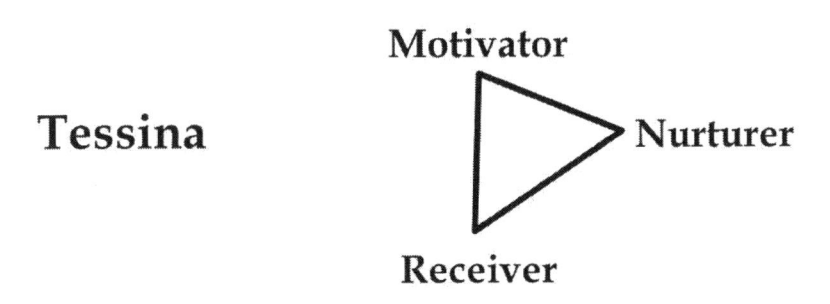

Tessina

Motivator

Nurturer

Receiver

As we can see above, the Victim is a Receiver for the experience, growing from the experience, the Nurturer is a Persecutor who still feeds on the Victim, but in a positive way, giving comfort to the Victim, maybe by force, but without taking anything from her, and the Rescuer is a Motivator who does not assume the action to save the Victim, but instead gives space and motivates the Victim so that she should act herself.

The Rescuer can feed on both the Victim and on the Persecutor, while the Persecutor feeds only on the Victim.

Unlike the Karpmann triangle, in this case there is a co-existence of the different persons, a binary contradiction, "I exist while I allow you to exist, as well."

There are no negative emotions in this triangle, but only positive emotions.

Tarot

The triangle that goes up, through real feelings, if the reader remembers, is like this:

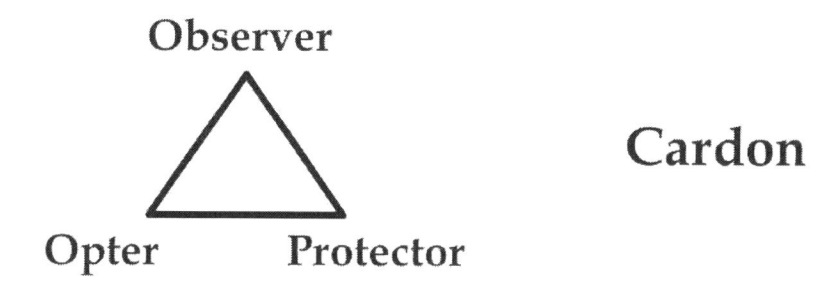

Observer

Opter   Protector

Cardon

- The Victim is a person that has possibilities of movement, which can be used in various ways.
- The Persecutor can just as easily protect the situation so that the Victim can act by itself in order to reach a solution.
- The Rescuer is an observer that can leave the reality to exist, by gaining more being.

In this case, the co-existence of levels is attained and a ternary contradiction is at play.

We can now make an analysis of the three persons involved in the situation, with each person having three possibilities of manifestation, depending on which triangle is at play.

In the next page we can see the illustration depicting the nine possible types of manifestation.

Opter

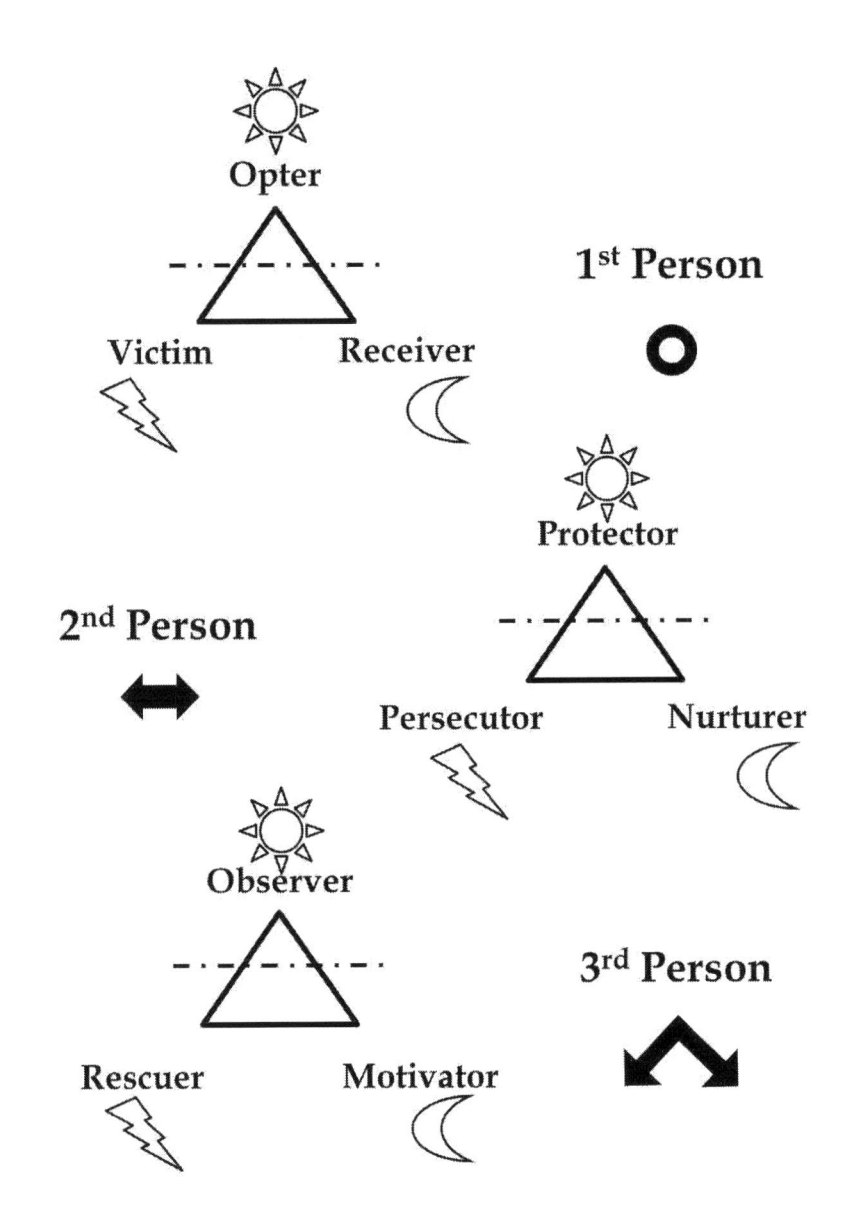

1st Person

Victim   Receiver

Protector

2nd Person

Persecutor   Nurturer

Observer

3rd Person

Rescuer   Motivator

If we use the following key words – Take/ Give and Active/Passive – we can gain some new understanding of the three situations we have just described, as we will have three types of actions: to take, to give, to give-take; and three types of attitudes: active, passive, active-passive.

For the downwards triangle, the Karpmann triangle with negative emotions, we will have:
- Victim: gives passively.
- Persecutor: takes passively.
- Rescuer: gives-takes passively.

For the horizontal triangle, the Tessina triangle with positive emotions, we will have:
- Victim/ Receiver: takes passively.
- Persecutor/ Nurturer: gives passively.
- Rescuer/ Motivator: gives-takes actively.

As we can notice, the lens effect when changing levels of reality applies here: Victim receives positive energy by force, Nurturer gives by force.

For the upwards triangle, we will have:
- Victim/ Possibilities: gives-takes actively.
- Persecutor/ Protector: takes-gives actively.
- Rescuer/ Observer: gives-takes actively-passively.

The actions are related to the energy – negative, positive, survival of the energy in another level (give-take), while the attitudes have to do with the level of free-will involved in each situation.

Now let's see the general map, including all the processes involved and with the use of tarot cards.

Everything starts from the horizontal contradiction between creation and destruction, represented by House of God card.

This generates an experience that can go downwards, upwards or stay on the horizontal, the World card.

This by itself creates a perpetual movement of the energy, Temperance card, which leads to the process of transformation.

If the experience is going downwards (fear, indifference, hate), we have the emotional fall, leading to the 6th process, The Devil card, with negative emotions and the classical drama triangle of Karpmann. There is only one being at play here, each person involved is fueled by his ego.

If the experience remains on the horizontal (courage, subjective love, detachment), we have positive emotions, and the triangle of Tessina. Here we have the being-to-being situation.

If the experience goes upwards, through feelings – objective love, faith, and hope – we have the process of re-creation (art) and the triangle of Cardon. Here we have the ternary-being situation.

All these happen in the environmental presence of card no. 13, representing Death.

We now have the classical six processes[48] explained in reference to the dramatic triangles.

---

[48] See also Adrian Mirel Petrariu, *The Mythology of the Energy*: Transdisciplinarity, the Force of Gurdjieff and the Tarot, Magisteria, 2015.

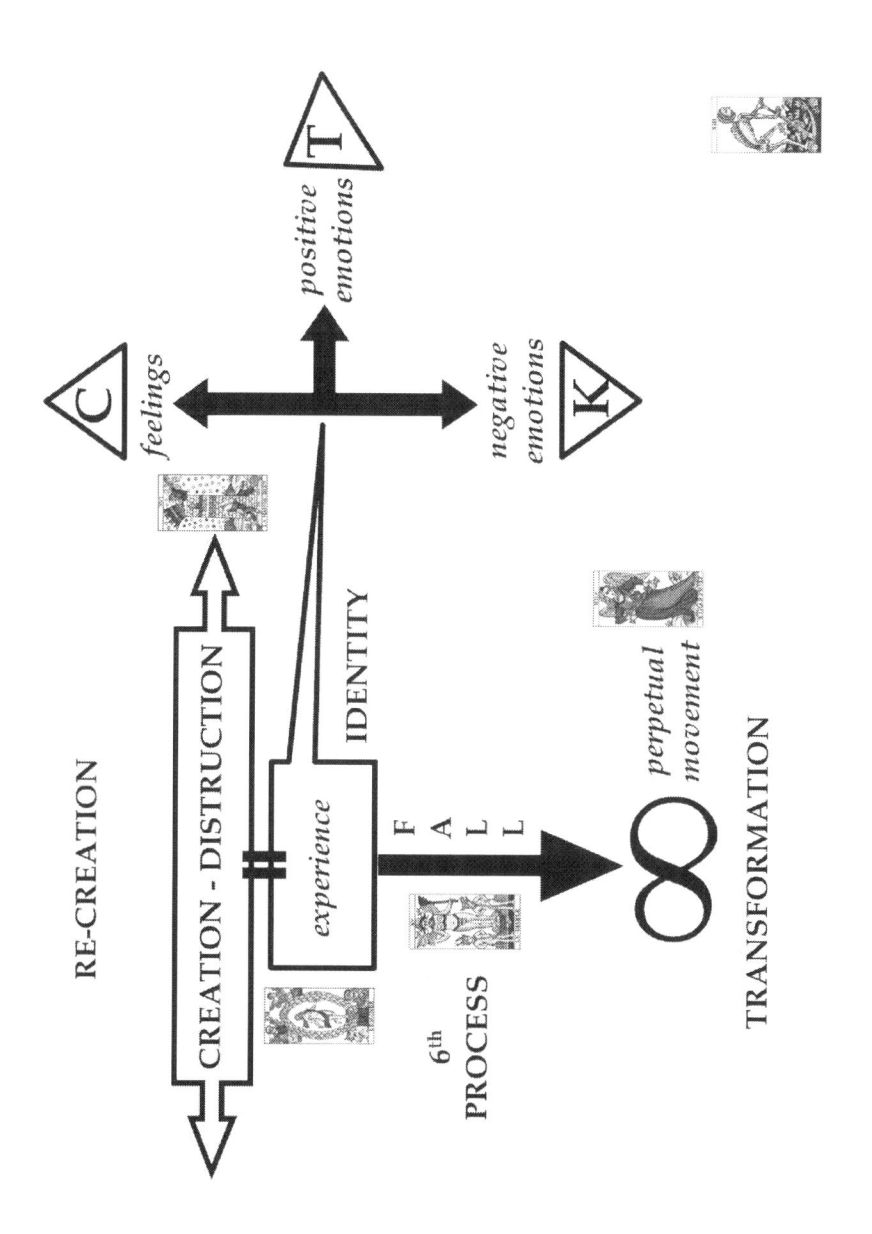

Tarot

△T *positive emotions*

△C *feelings*

△K *negative emotions*

RE-CREATION

CREATION - DISTRUCTION

IDENTITY

experience

F
A
L
L

6th PROCESS

perpetual movement

∞

TRANSFORMATION

As Adrian Mirel Petrariu posits[49]:

> In the ascensional triangle of relationships, the survivor of experience needs to be responsible for their own work on possibilities so it does not need saviors but protectors of their possibilities and observers of their actions.
>
> So basically, for these ascensions, the survivor of experience needs to be seen by the highest parent, God, in their actions and be together with others, having the contradiction in the social level acting as source of power for movement and protecting environment in front of Death.

---

[49] https://www.facebook.com/solmancer/posts/1732727580368375

Extracting meaning

In what follows, we shall see how the coach will approach the client's issue in order to use the tarot cards. The illustrations that follow should be used as food for thought.

Translating into symbols

At first, the coach should be able to hold in his mind different images of cards related to the client's issue. While not interrupting the client. For the coach, it is like translating the client's words into symbols and cards. This ability should be cultivated by the coach over time in the everyday life.

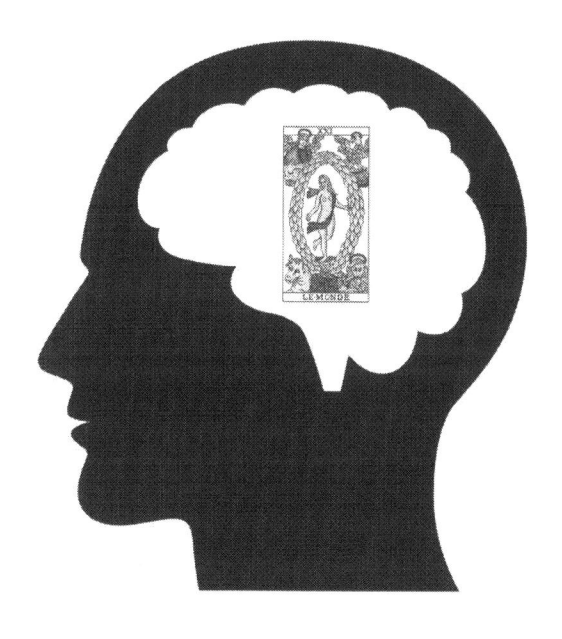

Frame of reference

The options of the client should always be seen as following the basic contradiction between Idealism and Realism and the coach should find a way to make the client see the situation as such.

The highest the ability to use formal and ternary logic, the higher the objectiveness in dealing with a situation from the part of the coach and of the client.

A Dialogue in Images

After the second session, both the client and the coach should be able to have a dialogue using the tarot cards as a conceptual tool for expressing their opinion and exchanging ideas and strategies.

The dialogue can be used with a particular frame of reference from the traditional coaching – such as the GROW model – or without. The coach should provide the necessary frame of reference.

The Map and the Territory

Following the famous saying that the map is not the territory, the coach should be able to extract meaning from three sources, as already mentioned: the map (model of reference), the situation of the client, the meaning of the cards.

However, no map is the territory and life is full of surprises, a fact as true as the law of hazard, and the coach should be able to manage incorporating this into the session, mainly by covering the basic option derived from the four dimensions of space, as explained before.

Moreover, the coach should use the particular meanings of the card that suit the situation described by the client and a relevant map/model of reference, either from traditional coaching or from tarot – a type of spread.

Conclusion

This brings us to the end of the first volume of the Transdisciplinary Coaching series, dedicated to the Tarot.

I have tried to present the information from theory at the beginning of the book to practice – at the end of the book, but no book can surpass the genuine efforts to understand the world in which we live and use one's mind, from a ternary logic's point of view.

I hope the reader has gained some useful insight from this book and I am open to any feedback that might benefit both the reader and me.

Good luck!

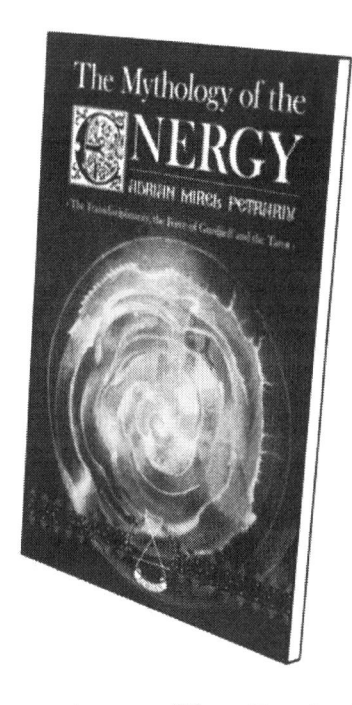

The Mythology of the Energy by A. M. Petrariu

Employing a literary language as close as possible to the mathematical and logical scaffolding of the Universe, the book follows the trajectory of the energy from nothing to everything and specifically to the human being that we all are.

As a Ph. D. holding degrees in IT, Law studies, Economics and Philosophy, the author has brought us this allegorical masterpiece, the only treatise where you can find, including but not limited to, the following: -How does the Universe work and by what laws; -The geography of Heaven and the Enneagram; -What is the Devil, where is to be found and why 666; -The origin and essence of love, falling in love and sex; -Missing fragments of Gurdjieff's teaching. And many, many more.

The Force of Gurdjieff, Vol. 1

A. R. Orage group talks as recollected by B. Grant and L. S. Morris

Orage is addressing both the theoretical and practical aspect, giving clear instructions of the Gurdjieff ideas and exercises which are missing in other published works.

Main Contents:

States of consciousness. The three centers. Forms of sleep. The catalytic center. Possibilities of experience. Collecting impressions. The three foods. Digestion and assimilation. Aspiration and inspiration. The brain as a stomach. The three forces. Positive emotions. Types of images in the brain. How to constellate. Vibrations. Types of relations. Emanations and radiations. Assimilation of air.

The Force of Gurdjieff, Vol. 2

A. R. Orage group talks as recollected by F. Schneider

Orage is addressing both the theoretical and practical aspect, giving clear instructions of the Gurdjieff ideas and exercises which are missing in other published works.

Main Contents:

Energy leaks. The six centers. The three foods. Verbal and formal understanding. Forms of mind. Degrees of Reason. Reincarnation. Essence. A normal human being. The seven classes of determinative circumstances for organism. The life review. Objectiveness. Conscious or Objective Morality. Good and Evil. Transition of emotional states.

The Force of Gurdjieff, Vol. 3

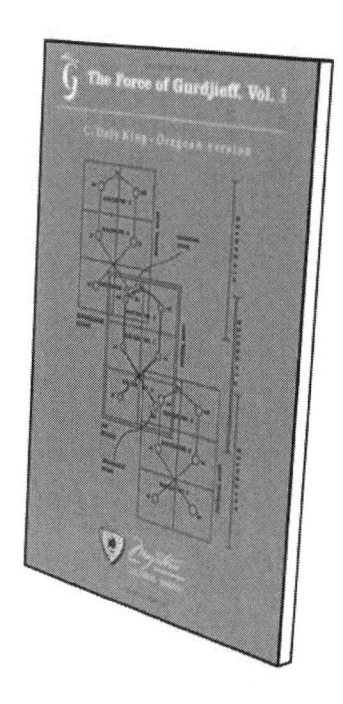

Oragean version by C. Daly King

A magnum opus written by C. Daly King - who received first hand information from Orage, Gurdjieff, Ouspensky - is now available for the first time to the general public.

Similar with Ouspensky's In Search of the Miraculous, this version of the Gurdjieffian teaching contains all the theoretical and practical aspects along with never before published diagrams and a coherent presentation of Gurdjieff exercises, transmitted only orally until now.

The only edition on the market with corrected text and remastered diagrams.

The Force of Gurdjieff, Vol. 4

Exercises

This is an unique edition where you can find - in one book - most of the exercises transmitted by Gurdjieff himself - in public or privately printed texts - and also by his followers, some of them are available to the general public for the first time.

Main Contents

The Two Portraits - The Time Circle - The Brain as a Stomach - The Globe - The Three Types - Life Review - The Nightly Review - The Gurdjieff Method - Self-observation - Participation - Experiment - Voluntary Suffering - Conscious Labor - Establishing constellations

The Force of Gurdjieff, Vol. 5

A. R. Orage group talks as recollected by S. Manchester

Orage is addressing both the theoretical and practical aspect, giving clear instructions of the Gurdjieff ideas and exercises which are missing in other published works.

Main Contents:

Politeness. Choice. Cosmic man. Self-knowledge. The memory film. Immoral act. Absorbing experience. Notes and intervals. Appetite vs. wish. Shocks. The chairs exercise. The etheric body. Forces. Chief feature. Seven features of one's face. Drama. Roles. Human types. Mystery schools. Manifestations. The three bridges. Impressions. Love.

The Force of Gurdjieff, Vol. 6

Gurdjieffian exercises by A. E. Cristea

This is THE book on Gurdjieff exercises. The author brings you a book which contain most of the exercises practiced in the Gurdjieff teaching along with new insights. A must have for any true seeker of truth.

Main Contents

The atmosphere - The "I am" exercise - Sitting - The centers - The last hour of life - Numbering - Eating - Breathing - Talking to oneself - Object details - Visualization of an object - One thing at a time - Self-observation & Self-remembering - Interference, participation, experiment - States of consciousness - Human types - Voluntary suffering and conscious labor - The nightly review - Alarm Clocks.

The Force of Gurdjieff, Vol. 7

Gurdjieff's Human Types by A. E. Cristea

Gurdjieff has used more than one system of human typology and this book explains, for the first time ever, the 28 human types mentioned by Gurdjieff in his books, The Herald of Coming Good and Beelzebub's Tales.

While this book does not contain all the information that Gurdjieff brought, it gives a fair point of departure in an adventure that will bring more being in your life. The reader should have a basic knowledge of Gurdjieffian psychological and cosmological aspects, as the information presented here is pour les connaisseurs.

The Force of Gurdjieff, Vol. 8

Gurdjieff's Enneagram: Origins by A. M. Petrariu

A fresh vision on Gurdjieff's symbol - the Enneagram - used nowadays in all fields of life is offered by the brilliant author of *The Mythology of the Energy,* **Mr. A. M. Petrariu, Ph.D.**

The information presented in this book is unique and the reader will have the chance to understand - through clear explanations and diagrams - the origin of Gurdjieff's symbol and its intricacies in order to begin to apply it in the daily life. A must-have for any serious seeker of truth in the gurdjieffian sense and one of the most important books on this subject written in the last decade.

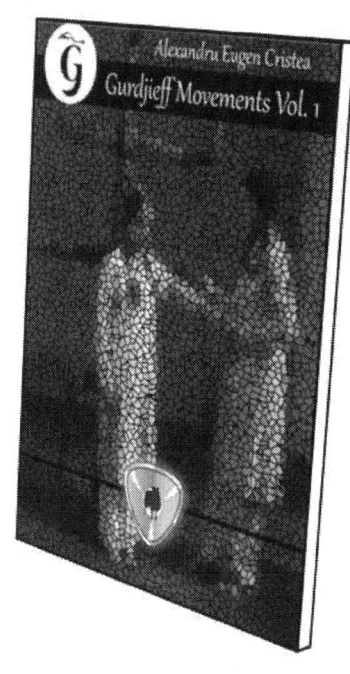

Gurdjieff Movements, Vol. 1

For the first time ever, the special Gurdjieff Movements are taught to the general public.
The introductory part about the Gurdjieff teaching and the movements concepts is identical in all the volumes.

Alexandru Eugen Cristea has made a tour de force in describing in minute details and photographs the various movements, dances and exercises brought by Gurdjieff. A must have for all the people with a strong interest in the legacy of Gurdjieff.

This first volume includes, among others, the Raising Arms, Canon of Six, Prayer, March and the famous First Obligatory.

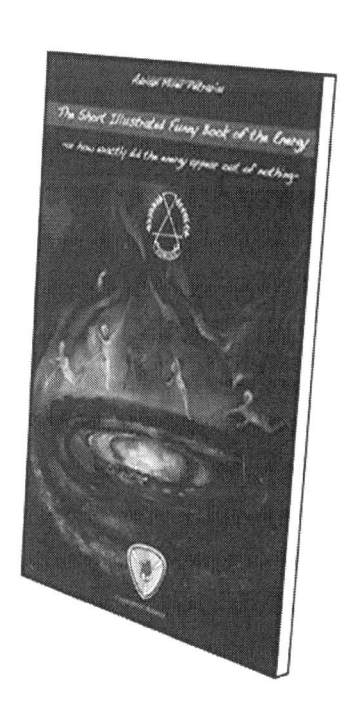

The Short Illustrated Funny Book of the Energy by A. M. Petrariu

Complexity is easy to understand: what is really complicated from a certain perspective is really simple from across the street. Always provided that one ever crosses the street.

This is a good companion to any title in the Force of Gurdjieff Collection.

Time is the greatest challenge of all, since it's the challenge even for Energy itself. Space is the answer to it, so by comprising as such the space of this divine story I hope the reader may gain time to live it. A moment of light will suffice.

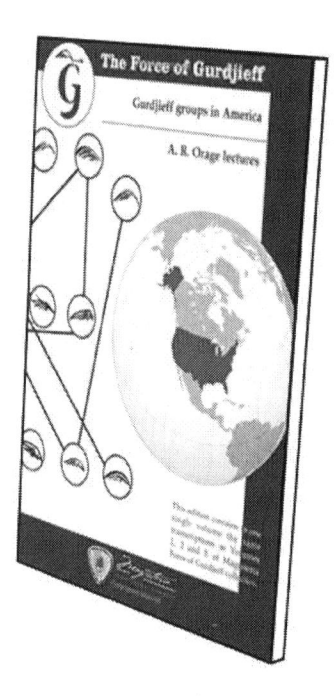

Gurdjieff groups in America

The volumes of "The Force of Gurdjieff" Magisteria publishing collection reunite various rare, important and sometimes unknown texts written by people who were influenced by the remarkable force of the Gurdjieff's teaching.

This volume reunites all the material from volumes 1, 2 and 5 in our collection.

While being the only disciple acknowledged by Gurdjieff in his own writings, referring to him as "my inner world essence friend", Orage was a crucial self standing spiritual figure through his own work and ideas.

This book contains explanations of Gurdjieff exercises.

The Cloud upon the Sancturary by Karl von Eckartshausen

The book was given a high status in the Hermetic Order of the Golden Dawn, particularly by Arthur Edward Waite and it is known to have attracted English author Aleister Crowley, to the Order.

As far as Magisteria is concerned, the book contains isomorphic truths written in a "extraordinarily simple language, so much that so that many may consider that he hides deeper matter purposely", in "simple fashion, one more suitable to the plane of intellectuality on which we usually are" as the translator of the book, Isabel de Steiger, has noted.

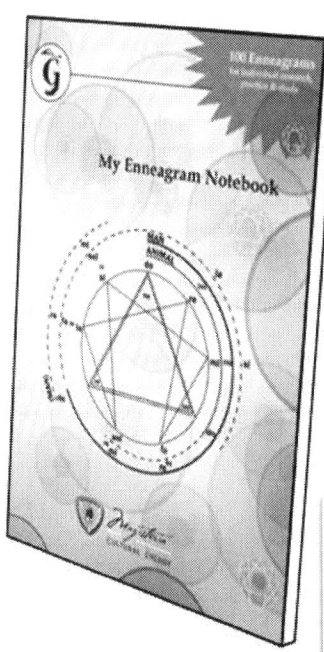

My Enneagram Notebook

This is a beautiful practical notebook, containing no text, but 100 enneagram patterns on blank pages, for individual technical work and discoveries.

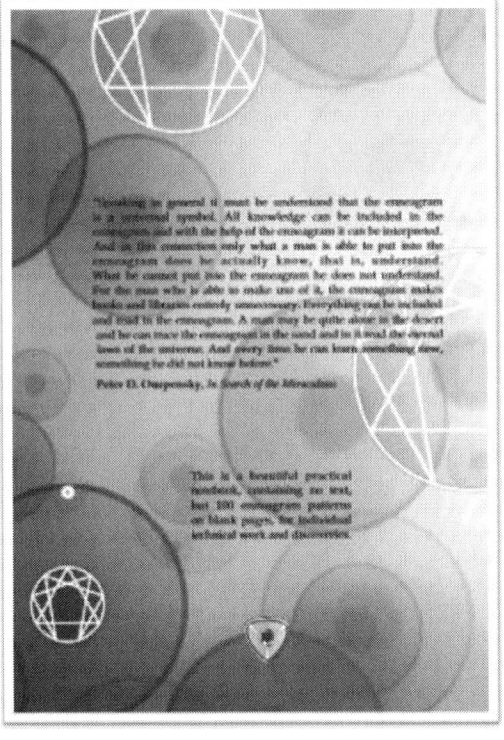

Flores del alma
Tudor Anghelescu
(guitar)

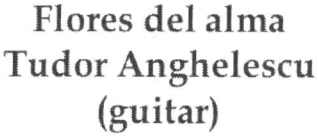

Tango sentimental
Diana Zavalas
(piano)

These are some of the finest interpretations of Argentine Tango available on the market, suited both for listening or dancing, as both were developed during tango parties.

A perfect choice for any season.

Tango Lessons
(book)

Tango for Teachers I
(book)

Kizomba 100 Elements
(book)

Tango for Teachers II
(book & DVD)

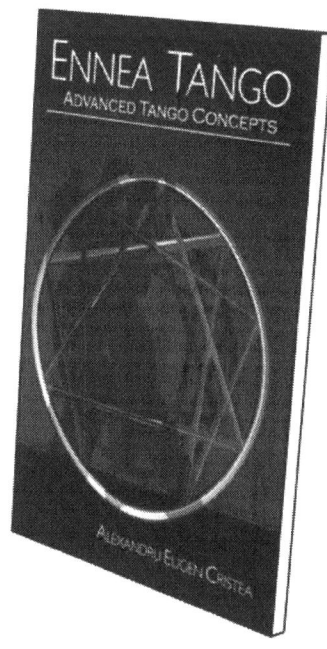

The only book in the world which has fully applied the original enneagram of Gurdjieff to explain a living process!

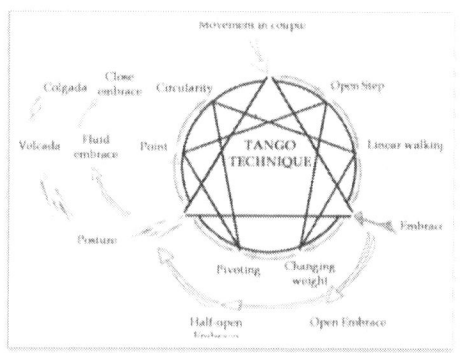

The Enneagram has become over the years a powerful tool used in order to understand ourselves and the world around us more deeply. Used by coaches and personal development trainers in all kind of situation – personal life or business likewise – it has become a trademark for real insight into the knowledge of life.

Magisteria
CULTURAL ENERGY

proudly presents a miraculous hidden world of wonders, treasures of amazement, heroes of truth and continuous enlightenment amidst the grey of inner uselessness and ordinary lives. In our endeavours we have brought so far to the surface unique items as the Oragean legacy from Gurdjieff, initially forbidden for publication, now available for the first time to the general public, the brilliant new general overview of the energy from nothing to yourself, forgotten sacred texts and many more.

Powered by: Artefaur

ARTEFAUR

Magisteria Publishing House is proud to announce our new partnership with Artefaur, the Romanian manufacturer of luxury apparel, craftware, amulets and souvenirs. Our collaboration pertains to the creation of objects bearing signification and meaning, able to help elevate the daily life. Soon our website will have a special section to this end.

Join us on: **www.artefaur.ro**

Printed in Great Britain
by Amazon